CRIMINAL AND VICTIM

CRIMINAL AND VICTIM
Crime and Society in Early Nineteenth-Century England

GEORGE RUDÉ

CLARENDON PRESS · OXFORD
1985

Oxford University Press, Walton Street, Oxford OX2 6DP

Oxford New York Toronto
Delhi Bombay Calcutta Madras Karachi
Kuala Lumpur Singapore Hong Kong Tokyo
Nairobi Dar es Salaam Cape Town
Melbourne Auckland
and associated companies in
Beirut Berlin Ibadan Mexico City Nicosia

Oxford is a trade mark of Oxford University Press

Published in the United States
by Oxford University Press, New York

British Library Cataloguing in Publication Data

Rudé, George
Criminal and victim : crime and society in
early nineteenth-century England.
1. Crime and criminals—England—History—
19th century   2. Punishment—England—History—
19th century
I. Title
364'.942   HV6949.E5
ISBN 0–19–822646–2

Library of Congress Cataloging in Publication Data
Rudé George F. E.
Criminal and victim.
Bibliography: p.
Includes index.
1. Crime and criminals—England—History—19th
century.   2. Victims of crimes—England—History—
19th century.   3. England—Social conditions—
19th century.   I. Title.
HV6949.E5R83   1985   364'.942   85-8923
ISBN 0–19–822646–2

Set by Grove Graphics
Printed in Great Britain
at the University Press, Oxford
by David Stanford
Printer to the University

for Doreen

PREFACE

IN the past five years, while preparing and writing this book, I have benefited from the services generously given me by archivists and librarians in Record Offices in London, Lewes, Chichester, Gloucester, and Bristol, and in the Guildhall Library in the city of London; and for these I am truly grateful. I am also indebted to Concordia University, Montreal, for a valuable financial grant, and to the splendid service given me freely by the Computing Centre of the College of William and Mary, at Williamsburg, Virginia; and among the faculty and students who participated in the project. I must pick out for special mention Professor James Whittenburg, a fine historian with a bent for computing science, and Dr James Lindgren, then a graduate student in history at the College, who can turn his hand to any useful task.

In addition, my special thanks are due to Ivon Asquith, of the Academic and General Division at Oxford, for editing a second book of mine with great patience and understanding; to Sheila Collins, of Marden, Kent, for typing the manuscript; and to Derek Blackadder, my student and assistant at Concordia, who has spent many an hour at such thankless tasks as checking numbers, compiling tables and generally acting as a factotum in helping to prepare the raw materials out of which the book has grown. And, once again, I am deeply indebted to my wife and companion, Doreen Rudé, for all her sympathy and forbearance, knowing that for her all these tables and statistics must be sheer anathema.

Beckley, Sussex   G. R.
August 1984

CONTENTS

ABBREVIATIONS

ADB	*Australian Dictionary of Biography*
Coll. W&M CC	College of William & Mary Computing Centre
DNB	*Dictionary of National Biography*
Glos. Pris. Regs.	Gloucestershire Prison Registers
Glos. RO	Gloucestershire Record Office
HO	Home Office Records, Public Record Office, London
London RO	London Record Office
MPCR	Metropolitan Police Criminal Returns
PP	Parliamentary Papers
OB *Proceedings* (or *Proceedings*)	*The Whole Proceedings on the King's Commission of the Peace, Oyer and Terminer, and Gaol Delivery for the City of London and . . . for the County of London.* London, 1810–50.
PRO	Public Record Office
R. Hist. Soc.	Royal Historical Society
Sussex RO	East and West Sussex Record Offices
Tas. Hist. Assoc.	*Tasmanian Historical Research Association Papers and Proceedings*
VCH	*Victoria County History*
VDL	Van Diemen's Land (Tasmania)

INTRODUCTION

1. PROBLEMS AND SOURCES

THIS is a subject which, in its various guises, has drawn the attention
of a wide range of social historians over the past twenty years. To
some, and among the most eminent, it has been the eighteenth
century that has provided the greater attraction: one thinks of the
distinguished work of E. P. Thompson, and of Douglas Hay and
J. M. Beattie of Toronto. The present volume, however, is centred on
the first half of the nineteenth century and thus inevitably owes a
debt to the pioneering work of J. J. Tobias in his *Crime and Industrial
Society of the Nineteenth Century* (1967), as it does to later books by
David Philips of Melbourne on *Crime and Authority in Victorian
England* and, more recently, by David Jones, of University College
Swansea, on *Crime, Protest, Community and Police in Nineteenth-
Century Britain* (1982). In addition to this work of an English orienta-
tion, mention must also be made of two distinguished contributions
to the study of crime and society in Western Europe: the first, though
admittedly not concerned with industrial society, is by P. Petrovitch,
the author of a highly original study of crime in eighteenth-century
Paris (1971), and the second by Howard Zehr, whose *Crime and the
Development of Modern Society* (1976) is a comparative study of
crime in nineteenth-century Germany and France.[1]

Each one of these authors has made a distinctive contribution to
the development of what has become a fruitful field in social history:
Tobias for his careful study of crime in the context of a developing
industrial society; Philips for making an early, perhaps the first,
attempt in English to focus on both prisoner and victim; Jones by
writing the most comprehensive work of all by embracing not only

---

[1] J. J. Tobias (as above); D. Philips, *Crime and Authority in Victorian
England, The Black Country, 1835–60* (Croom Helm, 1977); D. Jones, *Crime
Protest, Community and Police in Nineteenth-Century Britain* (Routledge and
Kegan Paul, 1982); P. Petrovitch, 'Recherches sur la criminalité à Paris dans la
seconde moitié du XVIIIe siècle', in *Crimes et criminalité en France sous l'Ancien
Régime 17e–18e siècles*, Cahiers des Annales 33 (Paris, 1971), pp. 187–261; H.
Zehr, *Crime and the Development of Modern Society. Patterns of Criminality
in 19th-Century Germany and France* (Croom Helm, 1976).

crime and police but also protest and community; and Zehr for broadening his discussion of the origins of crime to include political, social, and psychological factors in addition to the more strictly economic. Petrovitch's study, however, stands on its own, not only because he is concerned with crime in a pre-industrial context but because, with the rich sources of the Paris Châtelet available to him, he has been able to give equal weight to both criminal and victim.

And this is essentially what I have attempted to do in the present volume, thus departing significantly from the example set by my Anglo-Canadian predecessors (with the honourable but only partial exception of Philips) whose focus has been almost exclusively on the prisoner and wherein even the prisoner has been most often reduced to a statistic. My method and my focus will be different: as far as the available records allow I will attempt, as my title suggests, to strike an equal balance between prisoner and victim (more easily done in the case of the Middlesex assizes than elsewhere), and also to supplement (and I hope enrich) my statistical presentation of crime and criminal activities with numerous brief case-histories of the persons involved. Thus it may be possible, for this half-century of English history at least, to begin to tackle the old but little explored question, 'who robbed whom?' In addition, I shall be concerned with other questions, such as to reclassify crime in a more useful way (like Howard Zehr, I am suspicious of the traditional method, useful enough to the criminologist or criminal lawyer but not to the social historian, of making a neat division between crimes against property and crimes against persons); as subsequent pages will show, I shall attempt to reclassify crime in terms of 'social' or 'survival' crime, protest crime, and crime *tout pur* (meaning crimes of simple pecuniary acquisition or personal revenge). The reader will be able to judge for himself whether such a division is viable either in part or in whole.

My sources have naturally been chosen to be reasonably useful in providing answers to such questions: in this respect, at least, I have not departed from the practice of most historians. But, as will become evident, these sources have their limitations. One arises from the repeated caveat voiced by other workers in the field: that criminal returns are hopelessly inadequate in providing a full, or total, picture of crime,[2] both because the nineteenth-century authorities kept

---

[2] Most explicitly by V. A. C. Gatrell and T. B. Hadden, 'Criminal Statistics and their Interpretation', in E. A. Wrigley, *Nineteenth-Century Society* (Cambridge 1972), esp. pp. 336–40, 361–2.

changing the rules (as by the Acts of 1847 and 1855) and, more significantly, because of the long delay before full account was taken of 'crimes known to the police' as opposed to those brought before the courts. It is true that, in the case of London, the Metropolitan Commissioners of Police (as I learn from David Jones) began to make such a distinction after 1831; in fact in 1840, when they made over 17,700 arrests, only a little over 4,000 prisoners were committed for trial.[3] And even today, with all the subsequent refinements made in the detection of crime, a large 'grey area' of unreported crime remains, and the First Report of the British Crime Survey, published by HMSO in 1983, shows that the 'dark figure' of unrecorded crime for the preceding year amounted to rather more than four times that of crimes recorded or acted upon by the police or courts of justice.[4]

In spite of the enormity of this problem (and no longer the relatively minor inconvenience of some types of crime having at some time been transferred for trial to one court rather than to another), I will again follow Zehr in refusing to be intimidated on the very practical grounds that half a loaf is often better than no bread and, in particular, because the present 'half' (or even quarter) will take an adequate account of all prisoners tried at assizes or quarter sessions in selected years in my selected counties. In this sense, to attain a statistical totality of crime is not my object and the existence of a large 'grey area' or 'dark figure' of crime outside my purview becomes in no way a traumatic obstacle to further enquiry.

So to my sources which, as I say, have been chosen with some care in order to find reasonably convincing answers to the questions raised: 'Who robbed whom?' and 'who were the victims as well as their assailants?' First, I must confess that I have not attempted to consider the whole of England (still less the British Isles), but being concerned with brief case-studies as well as with statistics, I have preferred to concentrate on a little over 10,000 cases *in depth* so that names—and faces—are taken care of as well as numbers; and these are spread, unevenly in view of the varying populations, over three distinctive counties—Sussex, Gloucestershire, and Middlesex (virtually synonymous with London) during the period 1800 to 1850. My choice of counties has been determined by necessity as well as by convenience

---

3 *Metropolitan Police Criminal Returns*, 1840, pp. 6–7, 12–13; see entry for London/Middlesex records in this chapter.

4 *The British Crime Survey: First Report*, by Mike Hugh and Pat Mayhew. Home Office Research Study no. 76. HMSO, London, 1983.

and accessibility to records: London (Middlesex) was the obvious and only choice for the study of crime in a metropolis, besides having in the Old Bailey sessions papers the richest source for case-studies of criminals and victims in the country; Sussex is my present county of abode and is about as typical a rural county (apart from the inclusion of Brighton) as one can find, and has moreover an excellent set of quarter-sessions records for the period; and Gloucestershire has a uniquely comprehensive register of prisoners tried at both assizes and quarter sessions for the period 1815 to 1871 and had, in addition, at this time a fair balance of industry and countryside. (Lancashire would have been a more obvious choice for an industrial county of the 1830s and 1840s, but, apart from a short period in the 1840s, it lacks a long run of suitable records at quarter sessions.)

To summarize, the records used have been, in brief, as follows:[5]

1. *Sussex*
(1) *Quarter Sessions*: Order Books in E and W Sussex ROs at 5-yearly intervals 1805 to 1850; supplemented by Recognizance Books (QSZ) between 1805 and 1835.
(2) *Assizes*: Agenda Books 21, 23, 26, 28, and 32 from Public Record Office, Chancery Lane, covering years 1810, 1820, 1830, 1840, 1850; also occasional printed lists of prisoners.

2. *Gloucestershire* (in County RO, Gloucester)
(1) Prison Registers, 17 vols. for 1815–71 (incomplete for 1815, 1855–71).
(2) Sample indictments 1840–60 (very defective).
(3) Registers of Recognizances 1805–35 (useful for identifying victims).

3. *London/Middlesex*
(1) Guildhall Lib: Printed Old Bailey *Proceedings*, 1707–1913—with focus on 1810, 1820, 1830, 1840, 1850. This selection of years, though logical enough, is unfortunate in one respect: I miss the most notorious set of violent crimes in this half-century in London —the Ratcliffe Highway murders of 1811.
(2) London RO (formerly at County Hall, Westminster, now at Clerkenwell): (*a*) QS Sessions Rolls, 1810–50 (skimmed through only), including printed Calendars of Prisoners for 1846–50; (*b*) Newgate Calendars for 1820–50 (in OB/CB, registers vols. 4, 9, 17, 18).

[5] For a fuller description see Bibliography at end of volume.

(3) Lib. of New Scotland Yard: Metropolitan Police Criminal Returns (MPCR) 1831–92, concentrating on years 1832, 1840, 1850.[6]

2. THE THREE COUNTIES

The half-century that concerns us saw the transformation of large parts of the country from a predominantly agrarian to a largely industrial society. They were years, particularly in the developing industrial areas, of dislocation and uprooting and marked by large-scale Irish immigration and city growth. In the twenty years to 1841, 400,000 Irish men and women had arrived in the United Kingdom, and 2,700,000 further immigrants followed in the next ten. Like thousands of others—demobilized soldiers and displaced villagers—they were drawn to cities which were already expanding and even bursting at the seams. The populations of Birmingham, Glasgow, and Manchester more than trebled in fifty years, that of Leeds and Sheffield doubled, while London's, which had its own particular reasons for expansion, did something between the two.

The more traumatic of these results, with their disturbing social accompaniments, were clearly more in evidence in the rapidly industrializing North, Midlands, and parts of the South than they were in the less directly affected counties of the West and South. Our three selected counties are among these; but they, too, though less directly touched by an industrial revolution or the massive influx of Irish, experienced a considerable growth of population. This growth, whose rate varied significantly between the three, is illustrated in Table 1.1.

Table 1.1†

County	Population		% Increase (approx.)
	(a) in 1801	(b) in 1851	
Sussex	159,471	336,844	112
Gloucestershire	250,723	458,805	88
London/Middlesex*	818,129	1,886,576	135

* Excluding the Kent and Surrey portions of the London Division.

† *Victoria County History: Sussex* (London, 9 vols., 1905–80) II, 217; ibid: *Gloucestershire* (11 vols., 1907–80) II, 175; ibid: *Middlesex* (7 vols., 1911–82) II, 112.

[6] I am indebted to Dr David Jones for suggesting this source for London; see *Crime, Protest, Community and Police*, pp. 117–19.

The more distinctly *urban* nature of this expansion can be shown by considering the growth within each county of the more concentrated areas of population. Thus, in London, the multifunctional City of Westminster—centre of government, law courts, and commerce as well as residence—grew comparatively slowly from approximately 150,000 to 200,000 in those fifty years, while the largest of the peripheral boroughs, grew at a far greater pace:

> St Pancras from 31,000 to 167,000;
> St Marylebone from 63,000 to 157,000;
> Shoreditch from 34,000 to 100,000;
> Islington from 10,000 to 95,000;
> Bethnal Green from 38,000 to 90,000;
> and Chelsea from 11,000 to 56,000.

In contrast, the population of the traditional inner City, as it progressively lost its old residential character, continued to decline.[7]

Meanwhile, our two other counties, while remaining predominantly rural, also saw a development in urban growth. Gloucestershire, in particular, which, with the addition of Bristol on its south-western flank, became dominated by a city (and county) whose population, if we exclude its suburbs, grew from 40,000 to 66,000 in fifty years.[8] Of other towns, far smaller in size, Cheltenham's growth was the most explosive: from a little over 3,000 in 1801 to over 35,000 in 1851. (We shall see that this explosion was reflected in Cheltenham's rising crime rate in a later chapter.) The old city of Gloucester grew more sedately, yet more than doubled its population from 7,700 to 16,000. Among the larger of the old industrial centres, Dean Forest rose in the same period from a little over 3,300 to 13,500; and Stroud, more slowly, from 5,400 to 8,800. Sussex, however, remained more stubbornly rural and only really responded to these developing trends along its southern coast. Most dramatically at Brighton, whose Pavilion, Royal favours, and tourist attractions swelled its population from 7,339 in 1801 to 65,569 in 1851. Further east, Hastings, as a somewhat pale imitation, grew from 3,000 to 17,000. Like the city of Gloucester the two county towns, Chichester and Lewes, grew at a more moderate

---

[7] VCH: *Middlesex* II, 112–19.

[8] Bristol presents a problem: whether to include its extensive suburbs in its population or not. By the time of the census of 1841 they usually were, which would inflate the figures given here from 40,000 to 63,000 in 1801 and from 66,000 to 134,000 in 1851. But to do so would create complications, of which not the least is that some of the larger suburbs were located in Somerset.

pace: from a little under 5,000 to nearly 9,000 each. For the rest, the urban centres of Sussex remained large villages or small market towns with populations of the largest ranging between 2,000 and an upper limit of 5,000. Yet Sussex, as the more pastoral and less urban county of the two, had a larger acreage: with 933,269 acres compared with 795,709 acres in the county of Gloucester.[9]

Sussex and Gloucester, then, were strictly rural counties, certainly when compared with the almost uniform urbanization of London. Yet they differed significantly in geography, degree of urban growth (as we have seen), and in their balance between industry and agriculture —all of which, as we shall see later, bore some relation to crime. Sussex has long been divided—as it still is today—into two principal parts: the eastern woodlands of the Weald stretching from the Kentish border westwards almost to Horsham in the centre and to Eastbourne in the south; and the western region of pasture and wheat, extending through Downs and plain up to the borders of Hampshire in the west. In addition, there are two smaller low-lying projections on both its eastern and western flanks: the western extension of Romney Marsh, well suited to sheep-farming, in the south-east, and the almost equally flattened coastal plain running from Bognor Regis westwards beyond Chichester. So there are few surprises: woodlands, hops, fruit, and pasture to the east, and a variety of grain cultivation in the predominant centre and west.

Gloucester, on the other hand, has a further dimension and falls properly into three distinctive parts: into forest, vale, and wold. The forest is less compact than the Sussex Weald, being divided into two unequal parts: the long, low Cotswold Hills in the centre and the densely packed Forest of Dean lying across the Severn to the west. The wold is the large area formed by the eastern slopes of the Cotswolds and turned over to pasture. To the west is the county's great life-giver—with no equivalent in Sussex—the Severn, with Bristol at its outlet facing the Atlantic, and fertilizing the vale country formed by Gloucester and Berkeley. This great variety of scenery has naturally spawned a rich variety of trades and occupations. Above all, the county of Gloucester, unlike Sussex, continued into our period to have important industrial survivals in the clothing and woollen trade centred on a number of western industrial centres such as the Forest of Dean, Dursley, Stroud, and Wotton-under-Edge. The woollen trade,

<hr/>

[9] VCH: *Glos.* II, 175–87; *Sussex*, II, 217–28.

with coal-mining, had been an important feature of Gloucestershire industry in the Middle Ages and in Tudor times; but both had declined, and coal-mining had for many years been moribund. Yet cloth-making, a major offshoot of the trade in wool, continued to thrive into the early Victorian period. It reached its peak in the late 1830s when there were still 1,000 looms at work in the Stroud valley. But, soon after, in the face of modern industrialization and the challenge of new capital equipment elsewhere, fifty-eight mills were closed and only twenty remained by the end of the century.[10]

However, up to the 1840s at least, Gloucestershire, like its neighbour Wiltshire, still remained a cloth-making centre of some importance; and it is significant that when the 'Swing' agricultural riots spread from the east in the late autumn of 1830 the Wiltshire magistrates warned of the social and political dangers that might ensue once 'insubordination' reached the manufacturing districts and the clothing workers of the west. (Actually, it came to nothing as the two movements remained geographically separated and, moreover, proved to have little in common.)[11]

Sussex, unlike Gloucester, had ceased for many years to be an industrial centre of any importance. In the sixteenth and seventeenth centuries the forests of the Weald had been liberally studded with furnaces for the blasting of iron. The eclipse of the industry proceeded in two stages: through the destruction of loyalist furnaces by the victorious Parliamentarians during the Civil War and, more disastrously, by the discovery of coke-smelting in the mid-eighteenth century, which drove the iron industry to seek refuge in the more profitable Midlands and North. To mark its total demise in the South at the beginning of our half-century, the last Sussex furnace was extinguished at Ashburnham in 1809. Other smaller industries—or more properly crafts—lingered on, like the potteries and printing still flourishing at Rye; but, by and large, apart from the variety of services offered in the coastal and market towns, the only major mass occupations surviving were those connected with farming. There was, however, one interesting, yet short-lived, exception. With the widespread imposition, during the eighteenth century, of excise duties on every imaginable commodity the smuggler came into his own, above all along the Sussex coast; and he continued to do so into the 1830s at least. Then, however, the smuggler's activities became

10 VCH: Glos. II, 127–95, passim.
11 E. J. Hobsbawm and G. Rudé, Captain Swing (London, 1969), pp. 126–7.

largely circumscribed; for a report on 'The Disturbed Districts of
Sussex' published in 1833 tells us that 'since the establishment of the
Preventive Service [meaning the more effective prosecution of smugglers at quarter sessions], smuggling is much diminished; the diminu-
tion has had the effect of increasing the Poor Rate'—a sensitive point
to record on the eve of Edwin Chadwick's New Poor Law of 1834![12]

Meanwhile, the county of Middlesex, with its outer ring of farm-
lands, its teeming streets, docks, workshops, shopping centres, dance
halls, public houses, and brothels, and its densely packed houses and
tenements, presented an altogether different picture. We shall see
how far such features contributed to crime and what types of crime
took place. But one thing should be made clear from the start: it is
that London was essentially a commercial city and that, despite the
contribution of its docks and City to the furthering of the industrial
revolution in the North and despite its own involvement by the building of roads and railways, it was no longer the major centre of
industry that it had been in the century before and would become
again in the century that followed. Paradoxically, during a large part
of these fifty years at least, it was Gloucestershire rather than
Middlesex that reflected the first phase of England's industrial revolution. And, of course, this will become more evident when we discuss
the nature of crime in our three counties. We shall find that while
Sussex crime, outside its coastal towns and older centres of population,
was largely rural, crime in Gloucestershire reflected all the varied
economic activities of city, forest, vale, and wold, while crime in the
metropolis, despite its wide diffusion over homes, streets, pubs, docks,
and shops, was essentially and fundamentally *commercial*.

[12] VCH: *Sussex*, II, 206–10; J. R. Armstrong, A *History of Sussex* (London,
1961), p. 129.

2

CRIME

1. SUSSEX

IN nineteenth-century England, even in the days of angry protest, crimes of violence were the exception rather than the rule, and Sussex, a relatively peaceful county, was certainly no exception. By far the most common form of crime was larceny, or theft, either from dwelling houses, shops or farms, or (an important distinction, as it sometimes involved the threat of violence), larceny 'from the person'. In these different forms larceny regularly accounted for 60 to 80 per cent of all crimes tried at quarter sessions and fell to a more modest 35 to 50 per cent at the Sussex assizes.[1]

The closest challengers to larceny were two crimes generally—though not necessarily—associated with violence: burglary and assault (including, of course, the rising volume of assaults on constables, headboroughs, and peace officers). In Sussex, burglary appears to have been a later arrival on the scene, accounting for no more than 2 per cent of all cases at quarter sessions in 1835 but rising to 30 per cent in 1840 and 20 per cent in 1850. At assizes burglary was more in evidence, ranging between 8.3 per cent in 1830 and 28.6 per cent in 1850; and robbery, too (still often termed 'robbery on the King's Highway'), though insignificant at quarter sessions, played a more significant role at assizes, rising from 2 per cent of cases in winter 1830 to 7 per cent in summer 1840 and to 9.5 per cent at Lent Assizes 1850.[2]

So theft, whether by peaceful (as most often) or violent means, provided the constant pattern of Sussex crime. It is therefore of some interest to learn from our records what persons engaged in these activities most commonly stole; for the answer will help to throw a clearer light on the nature of crime in the county than we can gauge

[1] QS Order Bks., 1805–50 (the vol. for 1845 proved too illegible to be reproduced on microfilm). Assizes records in Public Record Office, London: Agenda Bks. nos. 21, 23, 26, 28, and 32.

[2] Ibid. For *assaults*, the equivalent figures are for QS: 1805–26.4; 1810–28.5; 1815–37.0; 1820–7.9; 1825–20.6; 1830–15.75; 1835–8.9; 1840–4.1; 1850–2.6: and, at *Assizes*, the proportions are much the same: high (20 to 28 per cent) in 1810–30, and tailing off to 2.6–5 per cent in 1840 and 1850.

from the simple record of the types of offence. We arrive at it by counting up the total of all items stolen in our 5-yearly sample of cases heard at quarter sessions between 1805 and 1850. The result reveals that seven types of item were more 'popular' with burglars, robbers, or larcenists than any other. In Table 2.1 they are placed in percentages of the total volume of theft in a descending order of magnitude.

Table 2.1. *Categories of Items Stolen in Sussex 1805–1850**

		Percentage
1	Food†	23.3
2	Clothing	21.2
3	Money and valuables (jewellery and silver)	15.5
4	Household goods	12.4
5	Building materials	5.9
6	Tools	5.8
7	Animals and animal feeds	4.4

* QS Order Bks., Sussex: calculations by College of William and Mary Computing Centre, Williamsburg, Virginia (hereinafter listed as 'Coll. W&M CC').
† Including 3.9 per cent for bread.

This gives us, of course, some preliminary idea of prisoners' priorities; we shall return to this problem in its wider context in a later chapter.

Such acquisitive crimes were as likely to occur in villages as in towns, though burglary, particularly in its more ambitious manifestations, tended to be an urban rather than a rural phenomenon. But, in purely general terms, it may be argued that crime was as much a feature of the village as of the town; and, in 1840, a year of considerable criminal activity, the names of as many as 127 parishes, both large and small, appear in the records of quarter sessions as having contributed a total of 427 cases of crime on both sides of the east–west border of Sussex. Yet, in most cases, the record of crime committed amounts to very little; so it may perhaps be more realistic, in order to arrive at a more balanced picture, to reduce the number of effectively 'criminal' parishes to reduce this total to one-third or even one-sixth. In the first, if we concentrate on the forty-five towns and villages that, during this period, attained a population of 1,500 or more, we shall find that some towns played a quite predominant role in terms of crimes committed. This was particularly true of Brighton, whose contribution to the proportion of crimes committed in these parishes rose from 13.8 per cent in 1810, still 13.8 per cent in 1820, to 20.35 in 1830, 17.3 in 1840, and 34.8 per cent in 1850. If we now go on to reduce the number of selected parishes to the first twenty in terms of crimes committed, the Brighton figure will actually rise in 1850 to a level of 50 per cent of all crimes committed. But this type of 'numbers game' is not such a good one after all, for if we take strict account of population—which it is reasonable enough to do—we shall find that the picture changes sharply and that smaller towns like Worth, Buxted, Battle, Lindfield, Cuckfield, and Arundel come into their own, with a record of one crime per annum for every 155, 175, 184, 247, 305, or 315 inhabitants, whereas Brighton, with its inflated population, can only muster one crime for every 556, or less than two crimes per year per thousand (a very modest figure indeed compared with the record of crime in large cities and towns today). Nor need it surprise us that, in applying this test more widely, the least 'criminal' of all the larger towns in the county will appear to be Chichester and Hastings (the first with a crime-rate of one per 3,212 inhabitants that year and the second with one of one per 2,366); for this is really an illusion as they both had their own court of quarter sessions independent of the county's jurisdiction.[3]

And now, to spare our readers any further statistical indigestion, let us turn from the general to the particular and examine more closely a number of case studies of both rural and urban crime. To begin with the rural, which in point of numbers at least, are the more characteristic of a predominantly rural county. Such crimes include the theft of flour, oats, hay, firewood, and hop poles, the larceny of farmyard fowls and animals, forcible entry, arson, trespass, and a wide variety of assaults. To cite a few examples, mainly from the records of quarter sessions, as these are both by far the more numerous and the more complete:

1. John Pankhurst and Robert Noakes, labourers of Westfield, stole two sacks value 10s., seven bags valued at 7s., and 20 bushels of flour valued at £10 from Stephen Orisford the Younger, a miller, on 2 June 1830.

2. George Stall, labourer of Alfriston, was tried at Lewes in April 1820 for stealing two bushels of oats (value 10s.) and a sack (value 1s.) from Henry Pagden, a farmer of the same village.

3 QS Order Bks., Sussex. Coll. W&M CC For further details, see Appendix A at end of volume.

3. In March 1805, William Russell, labourer of Newton, in West Sussex, was acquitted of stealing a hundredweight of hay (value 2s.), the property of Catherine Burwick, widow, and farmers Edwin Dunn and John Butler; while Charles Cutter, of Patcham, was sentenced to a month in jail at Lewes on 2 April of that year for stealing 20 lb. hay (6d.) from John and Richard Hansher, gentlemen farmers.

4. Firewood was a common object of larceny, particularly in the late winter months; and Robert Silvester and James Till, labourers of Treyford, in West Sussex, were found guilty of stealing 20 pieces of wood from Norman Shipley Mainwaring at the quarter sessions at Petworth in January 1820; while, in February 1830, John Venis, labourer of Battle, was jailed in the House of Correction for two months for stealing 21 hop poles (3s.) from Tilden Smith, a farmer at Penshurst.

4. Farm animals and poultry, including hens and ducks as well as horses and sheep and cattle, were also common targets of attack; and, on 19 September 1815, we read of Richard Florance, of Rumboldsdyke, stealing three fowls (3s.) from John Hall, a fellow-labourer of the same village; while, on 4 June 1804, Richard Hunt stole a mallard and two ducks (2s.), the property of James Howard, a labourer of Mid Lavant in West Sussex; and James Benwick was sentenced at assizes to be hanged for a far more serious offence —for stealing a gelding valued at £25 from Thomas Pearson and a mare valued at £20 from Harriet Baxter, both farmers of Heathfield.

Some rural crimes, like trespass, the extension of enclosures, and assaults on bailiffs and policemen, were often considered more 'gentlemanly' crimes as they were less often committed, or at least instigated, by common labourers or craftsmen. For example, it was William Clidow Esq., an attorney of Chancery Lane in London, who built two bridges across common land in order to link Ticehurst and Etchingham, both in East Sussex, and was ordered to stand trial at the next sessions at Lewes. Nathaniel Borrer, a gentleman of Hurstpierpoint, was also deemed to have committed a nuisance or an injury to common rights when he dug a ditch five feet by ten feet along a highway running from Boling village into Pickwell Lane, Cuckfield; and four Brighton grocers—therefore men of the 'middling' rather than of the 'genteel' sort—escaped with fines ranging between 20s. and £25 for assaulting William Crandon, the headborough of their Hundred, in November 1824.

Other crimes were more typically urban, such as the theft of jewellery or gold and silver, obtaining money by false pretences, counterfeiting and forgery, or larger-scale larceny in stationers', grocers', bakers', and general stores. Here is a selection of cases from Brighton and its neighbours:

1. On 2 August 1840, John Mann, a labourer, stole twelve silver tea spoons (value £2. 10s.), four silver salt spoons (10s.) and a pair of silver sugar tongs (5s.), the property of his employer, Joseph Parsons.

2. On 24 June 1830, Biddy Conroy, a singlewoman, stole two pairs of shoes (5s.), a pair of half-boots (3s.), a petticoat (2s.), a shawl (2s.), a frock (3s.), a pinafore (1s.), a handkerchief (1s.), and two pairs of stockings, the property of Johanna Callaghan, a widow.

3. On 7 August 1810, Mordecai Barnett and Lyon Ezekiel were charged with conspiring to obtain a large sum of money from John Fair, a Brighton shopkeeper, by false pretences.

4. On 22 October 1835, Matthew Taylor, a Brighton labourer, was charged with issuing a counterfeit penny; and at Arundel, further west, another labourer, John Warren, was charged with passing a counterfeit half-crown to Philadelphia, wife of Charles Chatfield, a baker; and, at Petworth, in July 1805, William Stoner, a labourer, was charged with attempting to defraud Robert Upperton, a draper, of the price of a hat by pretending to buy it on the credit of his master, Richard Smith.

5. At Arundel, too, Richard Knight and Daniel Breads, both described as labourers, broke into a counting-house; the property of Thomas Chatfield and George Grantham, of Lewes, and stole a large number of half-crowns and other silver coins, kept in a chest and amounting to a value of £5.[4]

Drapers' shops were the target at Arundel in July 1810 and at Pulborough in October 1820. At Arundel, William Lipscomb, labourer, stole a cotton gown valued at 10s., a cotton handkerchief (6d.), a pair of gloves (6d.), a pair of stockings (6d.), a small wooden box, and a metal medal, both valued at ½d.—therefore things of little

---

4 QS Order Bks., Sussex. 1805–50.

worth—the property of Mary Pearson, a widow; and, at Pulborough, Sarah Farley, a spinster, stole a gown (2s.), a corset (1s.), a shift (1s.), an apron (4d.), a cap (2d.), a pocket (2d.), and a ribbon (1s.) from Joyce Holden; and although the goods stolen were of modest value she was transported for this offence to Australia for seven years.[5]

Other typical urban offences were the receiving of stolen goods and the removal of lead from gutters and roofs. Among the first of these there was the case of John Ellis junior who, at Brighton in February 1814, was charged with 'receiving' three guinea fowls worth 10s., four geese (20s.), seven ducks (14s.), and fourteen fowls (28s.), the property of the Earl of Chichester and said to have been stolen by 'a certain ill-disposed person'; and, among the second there was the case of John Humphrey, a Horsham labourer, who was found not guilty of stealing 15 lb. of lead (1s. 10d.) from the roof of William Sheppard's house in March 1835.[6]

But in Sussex one crime at least remained the particular preserve of the Pavilion-city, Brighton: the keeping of brothels or of houses termed 'disorderly' or 'bawdy'. Three such cases appear in the quarter sessions between 1805 and 1835. In the first, John Morris, a labourer, was sentenced to a month in the House of Correction at Lewes for keeping a 'bawdy house' and thus 'causing a nuisance'. In the second, James Botting, a farmer, was charged with keeping 'divers disorderly houses' and ordered to pay a surety of £40 to ensure his attendance at the next quarter sessions; and, in the third, Mary, wife of John Turner, described as a labourer, was given six months' hard labour in the House of Correction for having, on 14 April 1830 and onwards, 'kept a common bawdy house in Apollo Gardens', which was visited by 'divers ill-disposed persons' (presumably these were the clients) as well as by 'women and whores' who committed 'whoredom and fornication' causing 'riots and routs'.[7]

There were occasions, too—though this by no means applies to the cases just mentioned—when Sussex crime, whether rural or urban, assumed an element of protest. This might be so (though for lack of detail we cannot be sure) in the frequent assaults on law officers and headboroughs—as at Ringmer in June 1835, when four labourers were charged with riotously assembling and threatening 'with menaces' Thomas Alwrock Bull, Poor Law officer for the Challey Union; or

5 Ibid.
6 Ibid.
7 Ibid., 1805–35.

when John Poole, a labourer of South Bersted, in West Sussex, assaulted John Frogbrooke, headborough and petty constable of Chichester on 5 April 1805; though it was less certainly so in the case of thefts of clothes from workhouses, as at Aldingbourne parish on 15 January 1835. Perhaps, too, there was a strong element of protest in the removal of steel or iron traps which some aristocratic landlords still scattered around their land to protect their ancestral estates against poachers or men of that kind. We find one such case, involving the Earl of Ashburnham, in February 1815; a second involved the Earl of Melbourne at Windlesham in January 1820, and a third the Hon. Henry Hall, Lord Viscount Gage, at Beddington, in East Sussex, on 15 April 1830. We find perhaps more certain indications of a collective or community spirit of 'protest' in cases of smuggling or poaching, though it would be unrealistic to include them all in this category without more careful examination. Perhaps we should concede the point in the case of William Legg, labourer of Northiam, who went poaching with a gun and was said to have threatened a gamekeeper who turned him over to the law; and maybe, too, in a number of smuggling cases along the coast running west from Rye, as in that in which James Whittington, a labourer of Pagham, on two separate occasions in 1825 (on 31 March and 15 September), was accused of flashing a signal to 'a certain person or persons'—presumably smugglers—in a vessel carrying contraband out at sea.[8]

Other rural crimes that on occasion involved an element of protest were the killing or maiming of cattle or fish in a pond, riots over enclosure, or the despatch of anonymous letters threatening landlords, persons, or farmers with reprisals. Among the first kind there was the case of James Wilmshurst, labourer of Buxted, who 'maliciously threw a bushel of lime into a stream', the property of the Earl of Liverpool, with intent to destroy the fish; but we do not know whether this was done as an act of vengeance or reprisal against the noble Lord or merely to provide a meal at his Lordship's expense. The same problem arises in the case of John Nelson, a farm labourer of Cuckfield who, in May 1840, 'maliciously killed' two cows, value £10 apiece, the property of Thomas Kermard, farmer; but was he the

8 Ibid., 1805–40. Smugglers operated in gangs and could be violent, like those who, in 1820, conspired at Rye to smuggle in 200 gallons of foreign brandy and assaulted two customs officers sent to disperse them with brick bats, shouting as they approached: 'Here are the bl–y–b–g–' (Old Bailey *Proceedings*, 1820, no. 344).

defendant's employer? And, finally, a more certain case of collective protest was that of the '100 persons or more' who riotously assembled at Maresfield, armed with axes, hatchets, and staves, to pull down a fence erected round a close called Shelley Arms Inn. The six persons arrested and brought to trial included a farmer (who, as first on the list, may well have been the leader), four labourers, and a woman.[9] Other cases, involving machine-breaking, arson, anonymous letters, and riots over wages and Poor Law allowances arose from the labourers' protest movement that convulsed the southern and western counties, including both Sussex and Gloucester, in the summer, autumn, and winter of 1830. To this we shall return in a later chapter.

2. GLOUCESTERSHIRE

In Gloucestershire, too, larceny was by far the most common form of crime at this time; and, as in Sussex, it was significantly more in evidence in cases tried at quarter sessions than in those that appeared before assizes. The comparative figures to illustrate this point are as follows:

1. at quarter sessions, 77.4 per cent for 1815, 85.4 for 1820, 82.7 for 1825, 79 for 1835, 80.5 for 1831, 87.5 for 1840, and 77.3 per cent for 1850;

2. and at assizes, 52.4 per cent for 1815, 55.3 for 1820, 51.1 for 1825, 43.9 for 1831, 42.5 for 1835, 44.7 for 1840, and 29.4 per cent for 1850.

Meanwhile, as in Sussex, crimes of violence like burglary and robbery were more often tried at assizes than at quarter sessions, the comparative figures being as follows:

1. at quarter sessions, burglary as a percentage of all crimes ranged between 2.8 and 10, with a mean of about 7; and, at assizes, between 7 and 23 per cent, with a mean of about 12;

2. and robbery, while never rising above 1.8 per cent at quarter sessions, at assizes attained 10.6 per cent of all crimes in 1831, 5.25 in 1840, and 6 per cent in 1850.

[9] QS Order Bks., Sussex, 1825, 1840.

So in this respect the position in the two counties was broadly similar.

If we now turn to the goods stolen in the course of burglary, robbery, and larceny—in this case between 1815 and 1850—we shall find that while the same seven categories of items remain as for Sussex, the order in which choices are placed has been changed. Table 2.2, which sets the new order of priorities in Gloucestershire against the previous order in Sussex, illustrates the point. It shows that the category of money and valuables has narrowly squeezed ahead of clothing as the top favourite, and that food has fallen from first to third place, and also that the proportion of household goods has declined considerably and fallen from fifth to last place, while the percentage of animals stolen has increased almost in proportion. (Yet we have to note that the two sets of figures are not strictly comparable, as the Gloucester figures begin with 1815 and not with 1805 and include goods stolen at both quarter sessions and assizes combined, while the Sussex figures, though starting in 1805, are not nearly so complete.)

Table 2.2. *Ranking Order of Items Stolen in (a) Sussex (1,507 items) (b) Gloucestershire (3,207)** *

(a) Sussex:	% of principal items stolen	(b) Gloucester:	% of principal items stolen
1 Food	23.2	1 Money, valuables	19.9
2 Clothing	21.3	2 Clothing	19.8
3 Money, valuables	15.5	3 Food	13.9
4 Household goods	12.4	4 Tools	9.0
5 Building materials	5.9	5 Animals etc.	8.4
6 Tools	5.75	6 Building materials	7.3
7 Farm animals and feed	4.4	7 Household goods	6.9

* Coll. W&M CC. Based, in Sussex, on QS records 1805-50 only; and, in Gloucester, on QS and assizes 1815-50.

We have seen that in Sussex in 1840, the number of parishes participating in some form of crime was 127 and that the number of cases recorded between them amounted to 427. For Gloucestershire for the same year the equivalent numbers were 144 parishes with a total of 456 cases brought to court, in this case to both quarter sessions and assizes. And, here again, the volume of crime tended to cluster round some towns or large villages rather than be evenly spread over the parishes, both rural and urban, as a whole. Whereas in Sussex it was

Brighton that, before proper allowance was made for population, emerged as the most 'criminal' parish in the county, in Gloucestershire it was Cheltenham, whose record of crime amounted to 17.4 per cent of all crimes committed in the whole county in 1840. But, more realistically, if we select the thirty-seven parishes and towns with a population of 2,000 or above, Cheltenham's crime record will rise for that year to 27.3 per cent of the reduced number of parishes, while next in order of magnitude will come Stroud with 8 per cent, Painswick with 6.4, Wotton-under-Edge with 4.8, and Gloucester with 4.4. Moreover, the number of crimes committed in Cheltenham tended to rise in each decade between the 1820s and 1850 in rough proportion to the rise in population: so that, in the 1820s, with a population of 13,396 (in 1821), the number of crimes committed amounted to a total of 73, and it continued to rise in each subsequent decade: to 169 (population of 22,942) in the 1830s, to 205 (population 31,411) in the 1840s, and to 127 (the only fall, but it was common in that year), with a population of 35,051, in 1850.[10] Yet, as with Brighton, it will appear that the toll of crime in Cheltenham did not actually keep pace with the rise in population. So, if we consider once more the number of crimes in strict relation to the size of population, we shall find that Cheltenham, with 1 crime per 136 inhabitants in 1830 (the highest ratio of crime to population reached), lay only in twelfth place in terms of the *rate* of crime and well behind the small woollen town of Moreton-in-Marsh with its 1 crime per 50 inhabitants in 1850, and also behind Painswick's 1 in 155 in 1830, Fairford's 1 in 79 in the same year, Wotton's 1 in 109, and a couple of others. Once more, as in the case of Sussex, there are some even greater surprises: Clifton, a thriving suburb of Bristol even then, with a record of only 1 crime for 1,504 inhabitants in 1830 (its highest point), Tewkesbury, with 1 in 1,240 in 1820, and Bristol, with its apparently almost spotless record —similar to Chichester and Hastings in Sussex—of only 1 crime for 2,035 inhabitants in 1830, its most 'criminal' year.[11]

Let us now once more look more closely at the different types of

10 Glos. Prison registers, 1815–50 (five-yearly sample).
11 Glos. Prison registers, 1815–50. See Appendix B at end of volume. The record is more 'apparent' than real because Bristol, though entirely dependent on Gloucestershire for assizes, had its own quarter sessions which tried 89 criminal cases in 1815, 207 in 1820, 154 in 1830, 287 in 1840, and 229 in 1850 (Bristol RO, Sessions Dockets, 1810–1850). But here, where Bristol is treated in a Gloucestershire context, it has been thought best only to refer to cases tried in Gloucester County courts.

crime in the county by citing a number of examples. Rural crime was similar to that in Sussex, though, as we have seen, larceny of food played a smaller part and larceny of sheep, cattle, and horses played a larger one. Among those who stole farm animals was Daniel Harrold (*alias* Weight), a 25-year-old ploughman of Dursley. He stole a male ass, the property of Daniel Tyndall, on the night of 21 February 1831. He had been in custody twice before, but in each case he had been found not guilty, so that he was given the comparatively mild sentence of a year in the 'pen'. James Lock, of Horsley, was less fortunate. On 5 August 1830, he stole a mare pony and, having been convicted at assizes before, he was sentenced to death for what still remained a capital offence; but, as usually happened by now, the penalty was commuted to a life term in Australia. Henry Smart, a butcher of Stroud, was more lucky. Having stolen three wether Southdown sheep, the property of Maurice Butler, farmer—presumably in order to further his own business interests—he was sentenced to death at the Lent Assizes 1831, though in his case this was later commuted to transportation for fourteen years. But James Hull, stonemason of Mangotsfield, was more fortunate still. He stole a sow (18s.) from the pig sty of John Smith of the neighbouring parish of Berkeley in the night of 22 April 1820 and, though found guilty at quarter sessions, escaped with a year in the penitentiary.

Ann Lloyd, a 35-year-old housewife of Dymock, was found guilty of a double offence. In the early morning of 27 September 1820, she stole four hens and a cock from George Thurston and three beehives from Richard Burton, the first a farmer and the second a labourer, both living in the parish. She had been in prison before and was transported for seven years. Thomas Cooper, of Chipping Campden, who was charged with the far more serious offence of setting fire to a rick of straw wheat, the property of John Horn, farmer (a dangerous crime to be charged with in the spring of 1831), was more fortunate. He, too, had been in prison before (when he tattooed a woman's initials on his arm); but he was found innocent and his case was dismissed.

Among the less common rural-type crimes (though this one was committed within the borders of a town) was bestiality, or sexual intercourse with an animal. At the Summer Assizes held at Cheltenham on 16 July 1831, Thomas Wood, 22, was sentenced to two years in prison for 'the abominable crime of bestiality with a mare'. But the bill against Mary Pearce, dressmaker of Ruscombe, for an even more unusual crime, that of administering 'an illegal herbal drug intended to induce an abortion' to the pregnant Hannah Crutchley, was found to be untrue. Another unusual crime was that committed by George Cowie, a Lancashire man then working as a window-glass maker at Dursley, who stole the manes and tails of four draught horses from the White Lion Inn, presumably to help him in his trade. The magistrates, who heard the case at quarter sessions in June 1831, do not appear to have taken a very serious view of the offence as they sent him to the penitentiary at Gloucester for only a week.[12]

Poaching appears to have been in greater evidence in the county of Gloucester than in Sussex and to have, on occasion at least, become more highly professionalized. Among the 'professionals' was Edwin Padbury, an earthenwareman of South Cerney; he had two brothers and 'all [reads his record] live by poaching'. Richard Cole, formerly a carpenter and 'a man of means', changed his occupation (the police reported) when he came to live at Little Dean, where 'he got acquainted with a gang of poachers'. One poacher, from the parish of Oley, near Dursley, was lucky to escape a verdict of murder; for when Benjamin Robins, 34, a weaver, was out poaching in the night of 25 February 1830, he assaulted and killed Francis Creed, gamekeeper to Robert Kingscote, a local landowner. But the court found him guilty of assault and not murder; so he escaped a sentence of death and was transported for seven years.[13]

There were also, as in Sussex, riots over enclosures and the killing or maiming of cattle. Two enclosure riots took place in the Hundred of St Briavel on the extreme western borders of the county, the first in June 1827 and the second in June 1831. In both cases pistols were used and prisoners were charged with riotous assembly, refusal to disperse when summoned, and the use of dangerous weapons, and, after a preliminary sentence to death, a miner in the first case and a labourer in the second were transported to the Australian colonies for life. In Gloucestershire, too, we find a clearer case of what may have been the killing of farm animals from revenge. The case involved Jonathan Henry Cotton, a shepherd of Aston Subedge, who, in August 1831, was arrested and charged with killing a ewe and two lambs, the property of farmers Price and Groves by whom he had been employed. But, in spite of the circumstantial evidence against him, the case could not be proven and was dismissed.[14]

12 Ibid., 1820, 1831.
13 Ibid., 1830.
14 Ibid., 1827, 1831.

In Gloucestershire there was also a rich variety of urban crimes; but this time I will spare my reader's patience and not spell them out in such detail as before. A few indications will suffice:

1. On 19 April 1825, Maria Silcock, a servant at Stroud, stole four promissory notes, ten sovereigns, and a silver plate from her employer, Robert Jacomb.

2. On 10 December 1819, Joseph Flower, a glazier of Dursley, stole a leaden pipe fixed to the dwelling house of Thomas Tippet Esq., of Woodmanscote.

3. Mary Ann Beans, 17, of Whaddon, in July 1831 stole a piece of white lining, two petticoats, and two pieces of muslin from a shop at Cheltenham. She had also, a month before, stolen a coat and a pair of trousers from Charles Digby Esq., also of Cheltenham.

4. On the night of 24 April 1820, John Hodges, 20, dyer, stole a great quantity of coal from the coal wharf of Richard Hopson at Stonehouse, near Stroud; and, a few weeks later, James Hulin, 45, of St Briavel, stole a cartload of coals from the wharf of Thomas Priest and others, coal miners and merchants operating in the Forest of Dean.

5. In May 1824, John Hall, labourer of Upton-on-Severn, was charged with the multiple crime of stealing a pair of boots and liquor from Richard Dawes' dwelling house, stealing a boiler from George Hemming, and a tea kettle from Joseph Garnson and two others, all residents of Cheltenham.

6. James Clement, 19, St James's, Bristol, also committed a typical urban offence when he stole a silver watch chain from the person of William Barton at Aust on 19 June 1820. (He was lucky to escape with a six-month term in the penitentiary: in London, as we shall see in a later chapter, he might have been transported for fourteen years or life.)

7. Thomas Staite, a labourer, broke into William Holland's dwelling house at Cheltenham on 25 March 1845 and stole 50 lb. of bacon.

8. Also at Cheltenham in 1831, Joseph Kettle, a servant, forged a cheque defrauding Messrs Pitt Gardner & Co. of £6.

9. On 12 November 1831, James Earle of Clifton broke into James Ivatts' public house and stole eight silver butter boats and other silver pieces worth over £5.

10. On 2 May 1831, Charles Elton Howard, a carver of Stapleton, stole from the dwelling house of Robert Pierce King, brewer of Berkeley, a £50 promissory note drawn on a branch of the Bank of England.

11. On 10 December 1830, John Clive, 19, of St Philip and Jacob, Bristol, assaulted Jane Curtis, a singlewoman, on the King's Highway and stole from her person a purse containing a £5 banknote and other money.

12. On 14 July 1831, William Smith, 24, a Londoner, assaulted Elisha Castle, a constable, in the execution of his office and forcibly released John Bull, a prisoner held in custody.

13. On 27 March 1835, Charles Skey, a bricklayer of Coberley, broke into a church and stole communion plate, an iron chest, books, pewterware, and other effects. He was transported for life for 'sacrilege'.

14. John Hepwood, a waterman of Tirley, was transported for seven years for 'receiving' two rolls of cloth and one of currants (£30), knowing well that they had been stolen from the warehouse of Humphrey Brown & Son of Tewkesbury.

15. On 18 January 1830, William Bidmead, a waterman of Stroud, embezzled 4 gns., the property of his master, Job Blick.[15]

What was referred to earlier as Gloucester's 'industrial' type of crime was mainly located in the western-central region of the county and based on Wotton-under-Edge and the neighbouring villages of Kingswood, North Nibley, Uley, and Cam and reaching north to the townships of Stonehouse, Painswick, and Stroud. David Phillips writes of the same problem in the Black Country south of Birmingham between 1835 and 1860, and he defines the phenomenon as thefts by industrial workers 'of amounts of coal, of pieces of metal and of tools, machine parts and manufactures from a place of work'.[16] In Gloucestershire, the problem was similar, though it appears to have begun earlier and to have been concentrated on the clothing trade and involved workers, and occasional small employers, who supplemented their earnings or raw materials by helping themselves to pieces of

[15] Ibid., 1815–50.
[16] David Philips, *Crime and Authority in Victorian England* (London, 1977), p. 180.

cloth from the gigs in the mills and of metal from their machines. Let us begin with a few examples from the Wotton district:

1. On 27 October 1824, Jonas Dash, a shearman, and Charles Bruton (*alias* Tanner), a spinner, were charged with stealing from a workshop in Wotton 40 yards of fine undyed woollen cloth and 20 yards of blue wool broadcloth, the property of William Freeman, a clothier. Freeman appears to have tried to recover his loss a few months later by delivering 40 yards of his own broadcloth in a cart to Joseph Roach, a fuller, then 'stealing' it back and charging Roach for the loss! Eventually, however, the matter was settled amicably and all cases were dismissed after hearings by the subsequent quarter sessions and the Lent Assizes in 1825.

2. Also tried at the Lent Assizes that year was the case of Henry Perrett, a clothier of Nibley, who had broken into Daniel and Nathaniel Lloyd's warehouse at Uley the previous November and stolen various pieces of cloth; and, in 1831, there were the cases of Joseph Knight, weaver of Wotton, who stole cloth from Messrs. Long, clothiers of Charfield; and of John Moody, a clothier from Frome in Somerset, who stole 14 yards of blue cloth from the house of John Tuck, blacksmith of Rodborough.

3. Also tried at the Lent Assizes of 1825 was the case of a cloth worker, who, at the previous Lent and Summer Assizes, had been found not guilty of first stealing and then of 'receiving' cloth but now was transported for a quite different crime: for stealing nine thick cheeses, fifteen thin cheeses, and three lumps of loaf sugar from John and Lydia Hewlett, shopkeepers at Frampton-on-Severn.

4. There was the further case of Susannah Daude, a woolpicker of Wotton-under-Edge, who, on 8 October 1835, stole 6 oz. of German wool from her employers, Samuel and William Alexander Long, clothiers of Charfield.[17]

The theft of metal parts was also centred on the Wotton district. The first case I have found in the 1820s was the larceny of a lead weight from a shearing machine belonging to Thomas Shurmer's workshop by John Wood, shearer of Horsley, at the end of 1824; it cost the prisoner six days in the penitentiary. The remaining cases may be summarized as follows:

[17] Glos. Prison registers 1825, 1831, 1835.

The theft of 27 top brasses by a clothing worker from gig mills in David Taylor's clothing factory at Kingswood in January 1830, followed by similar thefts from the same mill a year later: first of 'a quantity of copper pipes and brass cocks' in January 1831; and, next, of a further 27 brasses from a gig mill.

Two other cases followed in the summer. The first concerned Samuel Robins, a 13-year-old clothing worker of Kingswood, who was sentenced to a whipping and to two months in jail for stealing 7 lb. of brass from Samuel Bushell, blacksmith of Wotton; and the second concerned Lewis Rymer and Edwin Webb, respectively of Wotton and Kingswood, who were transported for life, after previous convictions, for stealing two cap brasses from the main shaft of a steam engine in Robert Darrett's mill at Wotton-under-Edge.[18]

3. LONDON

Crime in early nineteenth-century London, although it departs in important respects from that of the two rural counties of Sussex and Gloucester, also fails to correspond to the lurid picture painted by Dickens in the 1830s and 1840s and even to that depicted with greater journalistic sophistication by Mayhew in the 1860s. This is probably due to the fact that earlier writers on crime and fiction tended to have their opinions formed by too narrow a focus on records in which crime was made to respond to the needs of drama. Today, however, we have little excuse to follow their example as we have the opportunity to form a far more balanced view by a careful study of the Old Bailey Sessions papers (by far the most complete and most valuable source for most cases committed for trial in London), supplemented by a more or less expansive perusal of the London quarter sessions and (more rapidly) of the returns of the London Metropolitan Police after 1831 that have recently been studied more closely by Dr David Jones.

But to acquire an overall view of the nature of London crime we must begin at the beginning, that is with the *Proceedings* of the Old Bailey, which, aided by the Newgate Calendars from 1820, alone give a comprehensive picture—not only of the most significant crimes committed in the metropolis but also of the prisoners and their victims. To begin, as we did in the case of the rural counties, with the main

18 Ibid., 1831.

types of crime. If, once more, we start with larceny, we shall find a
picture not greatly dissimilar from the one we found before: that is,
that in London, as in Sussex and Gloucester, larceny runs well ahead
of all other crimes, accounting at assizes for 74.9 per cent of all cases
heard in 1810, 79.2 per cent in 1820, 83.5 in 1830,[19] 77.1 per cent in
1840, and then falling to 58.8 per cent in 1850. (Yet, as compensation, we find that by 1850 there had been a considerable transfer of
cases of larceny to the courts of quarter sessions, 90–5 per cent of
whose business in that year related to theft.)[20]

Among the various forms of larceny, the stealing of food no longer
attains the importance that it had in Sussex and Gloucester; at the
London and Middlesex assizes it rarely rises above 2.5 per cent of all
crime. In London there are two other types of theft whose relative
importance far outshines it: these are larceny 'from the person',
accounting for 8.8 per cent of all larceny in 1810, 17.4 per cent in
1820, 13.9 in 1830, 10.8 in 1840, and 11.75 in 1850; and larceny 'by a
servant', accounting for 11.1 per cent of all cases of larceny in 1810,
8.3 in 1820, 12.7 in 1830, 16.0 in 1840, and rising to the remarkable
figure of 30.8 per cent in 1850. To these figures and their significance
for the nature of London crime we shall return later in this chapter.

Meanwhile, let us look briefly at what had by this time become a
relatively minor aspect of London larceny and London crime: the theft
of sheep, cattle, horses, and fowls. For, although London had become
an overwhelmingly urban city (and county), it now extended north-
wards into such largely rural parishes as Edmonton, Tottenham, and
Enfield, westwards into Twickenham and Richmond and eastwards
into the townships and villages of Essex, long a 'dormitory' area for
the citizens of London; and such areas provided plenty of open fields
and rich pasture for sheep and cattle; moreover, the great meat market
of Smithfield lay in the heart of the City and thus within easy reach
of London's agricultural borders. So it is not surprising that we should
find, in these parts, particularly in the early decades of the century, a

[19] By 1830, this figure may have become an overstatement. As a witness told
the Select Committee on London's Police in 1828: '. . . if . . . it be taken into
consideration that, since witnesses and prosecutors have been allowed their
expenses, there has been a much greater disposition to prosecute than
formerly, I think that the increase in the Metropolis has been rather over-
stated'. (C. Emsley, Policing and its Context 1750–1870, London, 1983, p. 120.)

[20] OB Proceedings, 1810–50. London QS, Calendars of Prisoners for 1850
(giving prisoner's age and crime but not occupations and no details concerning
victims).

fair number of cases of larceny involving farmyard fowls and beasts and even of such crimes as destroying enclosures and maiming or killing cattle. Here are a few examples:

1. On 14 January 1810, James Robinson, an unemployed labourer of Tottenham, stole a mare (£2) and five fowls (6d.) from Anthony Aldridge, whose mare was left to graze in a field opposite his house. In this case the prisoner's poverty counted against him and led to his detection, as he did not have the 3d. needed to pay the toll at the Stamford Hill Turnpike through which he had to pass.

2. In May 1820, John Harvey and John and William Berry were charged with stealing a sheep valued at 60s. from Edward Boards, a farmer at Edmonton. The animal's head was found in a ditch a mile away, but the case was dismissed after it was revealed that the wife of the prosecution's principal witness had eloped with the prisoner Harvey.

3. There are two cases—one from May 1820, the other from April 1830—suspected of involving the malicious maiming of a mare in the first case and of a cow in the second. Both cases were dismissed as in neither could any malicious intention be established.

4. Also in May 1820, John Quinton, a butcher of Church Street Finsbury, was charged with stealing two heifers (£25) which the farmer, Thomas Lunn, kept in a field at Putney. This case, too, was dismissed as the prisoner was able to produce a convincing alibi.

Finally, a case of rural protest. John Steers and William Goodhall, labourers of Isleworth, in April 1830 removed and buried a gate which the Surveyors of Highways had erected in a field 'in some enclosures' to serve as a boundary between the two parishes of Isleworth and Heston. Both men were found guilty; but one, who was recommended to mercy, was let off with a month in jail, while the other, who received no such favours, was transported to Australia for the same offence. We shall see in a later chapter that such discrimination was not uncommon, and that it happened often enough that the punishment was not made, too strictly at least, to fit the crime.[21]

But, not surprisingly, these borderland offences did not figure largely in the sum total of London's crime. The heartland of that crime, of course, lay far nearer to the centre. We can locate it accur-

---

[21] *Proceedings*, 1810, no. 274; 1820, nos. 584, 761, 783; 1830, nos. 1174, 1202, 1248.

ately enough by counting up the number of crimes committed in each
of the main parishes and, at some stage of the argument, relating these
to the parish's population. To begin, quite simply, with the local
crimes as a proportion of the whole. The three northern parishes that
we mentioned (forming between them the so-called Edmonton
Hundred) rarely exceed, in any one year, a combined total of 1 per
cent. But, moving eastwards from Chiswick and Hammersmith,
Kensington has a range over the five decades of 0.8 per cent to 2.3,
while Chelsea, over the same period, varies between 1.2 and 1.7. In
the Holborn Division further east, there was St Andrew Holborn with
a range of 1.6 to 4.1 (but falling progessively between 1810 and 1850),
St Pancras with between 2.3 and 5.3, and St Marylebone, which had
the highest proportion of London crime of any single parish, with a
range of between 4.8 and 8.2 per cent. East of the Inner City we find
some important challengers with Stepney's 0.9 to 4.2, Whitechapel's
0.9 to 2.9, and Shoreditch's 0.8 to 2.6, though St Paul's Covent Garden,
in the City and Liberty of Westminster, easily surpasses these with a
range of between 2.3 and 5.8 per cent. Yet there remains the City of
London within the Walls, whose 102 parishes, clustered over a single
square mile, produced the highest rate of all: ranging from 11.7 per
cent of London's crime at its lowest level in 1850 to 21.3 per cent a
its highest in 1810, and with a mean for each of its five decennial
years of 18.6. This, then, is where the crime was most densely concentrated and not in the single, but vast, parish of St Marylebone,
whose population in 1850 had more than doubled in forty years and,
with close to 158,000 inhabitants in 1850, could have swallowed the
long stagnating population of the Inner City eight times over and
more.[22]

In contrast with larceny, crimes of violence played a somewhat
modest role in the record of metropolitan crime; it was only rarely
that, even in combination, they accounted for more than one in eight
of all the cases brought for trial at the Old Bailey. Table 2.3 seeks to
summarize the incidence of such crimes of violence as a percentage of
all crime in London.

Of these crimes only assaults appear in the records of London
quarter sessions for this period, and they rarely amount to more than
2 per cent of the cases brought to trial at any session; and even among
the 77,000 taken into custody by the Metropolitan Police Commis-

[22] For a table that illustrates these figures and trends in far greater detail,
see Appendix C at end of volume.

Table 2.3. Crimes of Violence, 1810–1850 (as a percentage of all crimes tried at the Old Bailey)*

	1810	1820	1830	1840	1850
Burglary	7.4	3.1	5.5	4.2	4.2
Robbery	3.5	2.9	0.1	0.4	0.4
Assault	1.7	0.3	0.5	3.7	2.8
Murder/manslaughter	1.3	0.5	1.5	1.5	1.5
Rape	0.8	–	–	–	0.8
Other crimes of violence	0.7	0.5	1.2	1.2	0.8
Totals	15.4	7.3	8.8	11.0	11.5

* *Proceedings*, 1810–50; calculations by Coll. W&M CC.

sioners in 1831 and the more than 71,000 taken in 1840 and 1850, only five, eight, and six persons respectively were committed for trial for murder, while about ten times that number (still a comparatively modest figure) were committed for burglary and robbery combined.[23]

Yet to the victims of such encounters the experience could be terrifying enough and they might well therefore have been reported—as with modern cases of 'mugging' in big cities—more widely than the bare statistics would appear to justify. As, for example, when James Sisson, a failed Hull merchant, assaulted Roger Parker Esq. who was riding home to Hendon along the King's Highway between London and Edgware. It was a real Dick Turpin affair although the assailant carried an unloaded pistol and went on foot. Yet he threatened to shoot his victim and took from him five silver dollars, a half-crown, a florin, and eight sixpennies. There was also the bleak experience of Jane Cox, a laundress of Bethnal Green, who was held up by three men on a snowy December evening on what was conventionally described as 'the King's Highway' (but was really Angel Alley, a tough quarter of Bishopsgate Street in the City of London) and violently robbed of the linen she was carrying to the laundry, consisting of two shirts worth 30s., a tablecloth, two handtowels, and a toilet cloth belonging to Richard Judkins and John Borland. A more recent case concerned Thomas Allerson, a publican, who was assaulted and robbed of his £3 watch and chain in St James's Square. The 'Mob' (as he described them) encircled him and forced him against the iron railings three doors from Lord Castlereagh's house. In these cases the

23 London QS Calendars of Prisoners, 1850: *MPCR*, 1831–2, 1840, 1850.

three assailants were sentenced to death. But James Taylor, who robbed Maria Crooks, the wife of a City toll collector, of a silk handkerchief, five yards of printed linen, and a key, and Mary Newman of
two yards of printed cotton in quick succession, was more fortunate
and was acquitted as there was some doubt about the validity of the
evidence.

Another case that was dismissed due to uncertain evidence was that
in which Robert Grew and Charles Smith, who frequented 'flash'
resorts like the Crosskeys tavern in Bell Lane and Wentworth Street,
in the heart of the Whitechapel 'Rookeries', hustled John Morgan at
the corner of Gunn Street in Spitalfields and snatched the watch from
his fob, having first struck him on the back of the head with a
bludgeon. William Sharman Wilson, who lived on the Old Kent
Road, was also robbed with violence when he missed his last bus home
from Hampton Court. Near Twickenham, he fell in with Charles
Dunneclift, a labourer formerly in the service of the Queen Dowager,
who, after drinking with him in a pub at Teddington, robbed him of
3½ gns. By this time the victim was drunk and later failed to give a
coherent account of what had happened in court. And, finally, there
was the unusual case of Edward Oxford, a barman of West Place, West
Square, who was charged with treason and attempted murder when,
in June 1840, he fired a loaded pistol at Queen Victoria as she drove
with Prince Albert in Constitution Hill on her way to the Palace. The
motive appears to have been political, as he belonged to a Right-wing
Tory group that was aiming to take power. The court gave the case
its careful attention: the trial took up forty-four pages of the Old
Bailey's printed *Proceedings*; yet it ended in the prisoner being found
guilty but insane and ordered to be detained at Her Majesty's
pleasure.[24]

But, as we have seen, such cases of violence were comparatively
rare. Far more typical of London's early nineteenth-century crime
was the rich variety of larceny that played so large a part in the Old
Bailey's *Proceedings*. One case, similar to some we have noted in
Gloucestershire, concerns John Robson, a carpenter lodging in Rosemary Lane, who stole a whole set of carpenter's tools from a first-floor
warehouse in Botolph Lane where Jesse Tupp, a journeyman carpenter, had left them, as he believed, for safe keeping. The haul
included two saws (12s.), four planes (12s. 6d.), a screwdriver (9d.), a

24 *Proceedings*, 1810, nos. 262, 408, 430–1; 1830, no. 1312; 1840, pp. 464–1510;
1850, no. 1112.

pair of pincers (18*d*.), a square (18*d*.), four chisels (2*s*. 6*d*.), an oil stone (3*s*.), and a mallet (4*d*.), to a total of 34*s*. 9*d*.

A more exotic story involved a merchant, Jacques-Alexandre Carrol, and a farmer, Alex-André Vitemont, who were convicted of illegally importing 200 black slaves into Mauritius, 'an island governed by the United Kingdom'. Another somewhat unusual incident raised the possibility of 'sacrilege'. According to the law, it was sacrilege to steal three yards of baize (4*s*.), three gallons of wine (20*s*.), 24 bottles (2*s*.), a box (5*s*.), 6 lb. candles (3*s*.), and a looking glass (7*s*.) from the vestry of a Church of England chapel, as Thomas Newby did at Stepney in 1820. But when, in September 1830, Philip Phillips, of Rosemary Lane, stole a gown worth £2 and two sets of robes (£24) belonging to the Revd Andrew Reed, a minister of the Congregational Church in Cannon Street, he was found guilty of larceny but 'not sacrilegiously', as there had been no injury done to the Established Church.[25]

Among common crimes in London were stealing pint pots in public houses and stripping lead from buildings, as we also saw done in Gloucestershire. In the night of 25–6 August 1830, Andrew Mann, William Lemon and Peter Gray stole 300 lb. of lead (26*s*.) fixed to J. H. Tritton's dwelling house at 46 Mortimer Street, St Marylebone, for which they were transported to Australia for seven years; and, in August 1850, a sweep and three sailors removed 630 lb. of metal piping and a pump (together valued at £15) from the docks at Poplar. Meanwhile, in April 1810, Daniel George had taken three pewter pots from three separate pubs in Marylebone High Street; and Henry William Miles, proprietor of *The Volunteer* in Upper Baker Street, which became famous a century later for its swearing parrot, had been robbed of a bill of exchange for £53. 9*s*. 6*d*.

Another common crime, though calling for particular skills, was the forgery of banknotes or bills of exchange and passing them on to unsuspecting tradesmen with a view of defrauding them, or the Government, or the Bank of England. This combined activity of forgery and fraud accounted for 0.77 per cent of all cases heard at Assizes in 1810, 5.7 per cent in 1820, 1.3 in 1830, 3.0 in 1840, and rising to a peak of 7.7 per cent in 1850. Sometimes defendants charged with this offence followed one another in rapid succession in court; at other times the court tried twenty or more cases at a single sitting—as

25 *Proceedings*, 1820, no. 275; 1830, nos. 1258, 1954.

when twenty-one defendants pleaded guilty of having in their possession a quantity of Bank of England notes, well knowing that they
were forged, and were transported for fourteen years. But when
George Stewart, an engraver, and twenty-five others were committed
on the same charge a few months later, the prosecutor surprised the
court at a certain stage of the proceedings by refusing to present
further evidence; so the case was dropped.[26]

London being a great centre of communications, it is not surprising
that common crimes included larceny on coaches and buses (though
not yet on trains) and on river craft and ships from overseas that
docked in the Thames. In April 1820 William McDonald was sentenced to seven years' transportation for stealing a coach glass, the
property of Lynch White, a livery stable keeper; it appears to have
been taken on an evening coach ride to Covent Garden Theatre. On
this occasion, one of the prisoner's accomplices (he escaped arrest)
asked rudely as the constable came up to seize his prisoners 'What
does that b–l–dy b–g–r want?' When James Carter, of Lisson Grove,
Paddington, arrived at Castle Street, City Road, by the Paddington
stage, he was drunk, missed his step, and fell on the footpath where
he was robbed of his watch before he could be put back on a bus to
the Barbican. In December 1840, John Wells, a pawnbroker, and
his wife Jane, of Upper Phillimore Place, Kensington, were also
robbed on a bus—in this case of £16 1s. in notes and coin; they had
picked up the bus near a bank in Piccadilly and went on to Bond
Street and Sloane Street before alighting, and were robbed on the
way. In September 1830, Edward Tierney, a cabin boy on the *Boston
Cutter*, stole eight waistcoats (£8), five coats (£20), and four pairs of
trousers (£4), the property of Charles David Gass, the ship's master, as
the vessel lay in London Dock. Unfortunately, the young thief fancied
himself in his new fine clothes and displayed them nightly at the
Three Crowns hostelry, which led to his arrest and conviction.

The barges on the Thames also afforded opportunities for simple
larceny; in May 1810 two watermen, Leonard West and William
Vincent, stole a coat (£1), two coats (£3), two handkerchiefs (2s.), and
three banknotes (£5) from a barge at Weybridge, the property of
James Keene, bargeman, and his brother John. And, finally, a tale of
crime and adventure on the high seas: in this case on the *Wales*, a
Chinaman sailing from Ceylon to London in the spring and summer

---

[26] *Proceedings*, 1810, nos. 249, 367, 493; 1830, nos. 504, 1060, 1209, 1954.

of 1850. The victim, here described as a 'poor lady', Caroline Pereira, a native of Ceylon who had spent twelve years in the service of the Governor, Sir Edward Barnes, caught the ship at Madras and enrolled on board as a nursemaid to the Darwood family; she also entrusted her jewellery, four pairs of eardrops, and ten brooches, valued at £405. 6s. and £99 respectively, to Patrick Smith, a musician, and his wife Sarah, who were masquerading as 'Lord' and 'Lady' Smith, to smuggle ashore; but they refused to hand it back on arrival. The two Smiths were found not guilty, probably because their credibility appeared greater than the 'poor lady's'; and, to add further spice to the tale, their alleged victim was later charged at the Old Bailey with having stolen the same goods on the high seas from her new employers, the Darwoods.[27]

But for crimes most characteristic of London in the early nineteenth century we have to return to the all-pervading crime of larceny, and specifically to that part of it labelled in the court records either 'larceny by a servant' or 'larceny from the person'—in short, to 'inside jobs' committed by servants, lodgers, shopmen, clerks, and to larceny by pickpockets and prostitutes. Between them, as we saw before, these two forms of larceny amounted to 20 to 25 per cent, or even more, of all the larcenies tried at assizes between 1810 and 1850. Thus in 1810, 11.7 per cent of larceny was committed by a 'servant' (a term that might apply to any employee living in the victim's house or working in his shop or other business) and 8.2 per cent was taken 'from the person'; in 1820, 'servants' accounted for 8.3 per cent and 'personal' theft for 17.4; in 1830, for 12.7 and 13.9; in 1840 for 16 and 10.8 per cent; and, in 1850, when 30.8 per cent of all larceny was committed by 'servants' and 11.8 per cent represented theft 'from the person', they reached a combined total of over two in five.

Most commonly the 'inside jobs' were performed by servants or lodgers, who gained access to the house and its contents by spending a short term of employment there, or by renting a room for a few shillings a week, before choosing a favourable moment for removing sheets, clothing, and furniture to deposit at the pawnbroker's down the street. Thus, in 1810, James Harvard, a servant, took two sheets (14s.), two tablecloths (12s.), one apron (1s.), two shifts (5s.), and a petticoat (2s.) down from the clothes-line where they were hanging to dry, the property of his employers, Rees Griffiths, an oil man, and

27 *Proceedings*, 1820, p. 420; 1830, no. 1013; 1840, no. 504; 1850, pp. 148–63.

his wife Amelia, of Paddington Street, St Marylebone. Elizabeth Scott, in June of the same year, came to lodge in William Kenny's house in Whitecross Street, in the City of London, for 4s. 6d. a week; but she left after four nights, taking with her a quilt (2s. 6d.) and two sheets (3s.). Another lodger, Maria Smith, a widow, took a room with Emma Vickerman, a singlewoman, living in Daniel Lynn's house in Tash Stret, Gray's Inn Lane. After three nights she broke the padlock to her victim's room and took away a scarf (£2), two shawls (50s.), a bonnet (£5), and three petticoats (15s.). Oddly enough, the defendant thought it useful to justify her precipitate departure by citing the 'immoral conduct' of her victim, alleged to have brought in a man to keep her company at night.

Sometimes the 'inside job' was performed by an employee in a shop, an office, or warehouse. Henry Walker who, in November 1850, pocketed £25. 4s. 2d. in toll money, worked for Abraham Redon, a tollgate collector at Cambridge Heath; he told the court that he and three others had borrowed the money to pay for beer. John Summerford, a records clerk at the Admiralty, also found opportunities for removing packets of sugar and books from the garrets adjoining his office; and it was said that he had, over a period of two years, been removing these packets in 28-lb. bundles wrapped in handkerchiefs which he sold outside at 4d. a pound. A somewhat similar case was that of Charles John Preece and Thomas Evans, customs officers employed as weighers in a tobacco warehouse in the London docks, who, in 1830, stole 6 lb. 12 oz. of tobacco (5s.), the property of HM the King.[28]

At other times the offender might breach the defences of house or shop by stealth or by enlisting the help of accomplices from 'inside'. Robert Anderson, who stole a watch (£3), a seal (2s.), and a bed-book (1s.) from a coal merchant's house in Golding Street, Westminster, had walked into the victim's shop next door to ask the price of charcoal and later, when the shop closed, had walked through into the parlour adjoining where the watch, as was common practice, was hanging over the fireplace by a nail.[29] Similarly, Thomas Stevens, a jeweller, who stole 12 yards of woollen cloth from Henry James Brooke's count-

[28] *Proceedings*, 1820, nos. 240, 294, 432; 1830, nos. 804–8; 1850, nos. 1, 842, 2096.
[29] In another case, a watch, hanging in the parlour from the mantelpiece, was stolen by a stranger who walked in while the wife 'was shaking out the tea-pot' (*Proceedings*, 1820, no. 1110).

ing house in St Stephen Coleman Street, had the task made easier for him by having been provided with a key to the house. And John Barnes, a former footman to the Marquess of Bath at 6 Grosvenor Square, found it less exacting to rob the premises of 61 silver plates (valued at £400) because he was familiar with the house and its inmates. He told the court frankly that 'the plate was kept in a strong stone closet in the pantry; the pantry door opens with a secret spring and bolt'. 'Was he in the house when the larceny was committed?' 'Oh yes, he was *below.*' (The whole story, in fact, is an excellent account of 'Upstairs-Downstairs' living in a late-Georgian household in St George's Hanover Square.)[30]

Larceny 'from the person' in London at this time took two principal forms. One was the robbery of sleeping or drunken sailors or strangers to town by prostitutes, sometimes working in groups of two or three (at times with a pimp thrown in), in the courts and alleys of Westminster, St Giles-in-the-Fields, or in the dockland of Whitechapel or Stepney (one such report speaks of 'the great many women about Whitechapel'). A few examples will suffice. In December 1810, John Tagny, a tailor of Chandos Street, after spending the night in a coffee shop, fell in with Margaret Graham in New Road Court and accompanied her to Vine Street to drink gin—the usual refreshment offered —and bed; she was later accused of stealing his watch (£3), but he was too drunk, as often happened in such cases, to sustain his charge. In September 1820, John Ellis Salmon, a cabinet-maker from Manchester Square, wandered into High Street, St Giles at midnight, where (he alleged) three women accosted him, all of whom lived together in Maynard Street. According to his story, he gave each one 1s. to buy gin, admonished one on 'her situation', and took another to her room where he was robbed of his watch and seal. But he, too, failed to convince the court of his credibility and the case was dismissed. A third case concerns Timothy Hall, a higgler from Wisbech, who drank gin with two young women whom he met at a theatre door in Whitechapel, went up to a room where he gave them each 2s. 6d., but subsequently lost his watch, valued at 10s. This time the charge stuck and the two women were transported for life. In a fourth case, John Johnson, a sea captain from Norfolk and master of the *Lively*, was robbed by two women and a man he met in Rosemary Lane, Whitechapel; the purse he was robbed of contained £33. 9s. A woman and

30 *Proceedings*, 1840, no. 1226.

a man, Hannah Brown and Cornelius Quinlan, were found guilty of the crime and were sent to Australia for fourteen years.[31]

And so we come to the most characteristic of all London crimes of the day, as immortalized by Dickens in his picture of the Artful Dodger and his young band of purse-snatchers. The picking of pockets had, by this time, in fact, become almost a professional art and, as we shall see in a later chapter, it was punished with great severity. Occasionally the pickpocket operated on his own, though then he could only hope for smaller pickings and ran a greater risk of being caught. In July 1810, William Russell and Joseph Willis, both 19 years old, each stalked his own particular prey—Charles Green, a super-annuated warrant officer in the first case, and William Youard, a carrier, in the second—across Westminster Bridge, where their victims stopped to watch the 'rowing match' that was going by between four and five that afternoon. In January 1820, William Brett (18) and William Woodcock (19) followed an unnamed gentleman along the Strand to Charing Cross, where Brett stole his handkerchief and passed it on to his companion. In December of that year, another unknown victim was stalked by a veritable Faginite trio, two older boys of seventeen and eighteen and a smaller, but nimble-fingered, apprentice—down the Strand and Fleet Street and up to Serjeant's Inn. They 'picked the gentleman's pocket', reported a police witness, 'within four yards of the Inn Gate which lies in the County'. Another police witness, who watched pickpockets at work in the City at the height of the agitation attending Queen Caroline's visit to London (see below), described one operation as follows:

I saw the prisoners and a larger boy; they were acting under his directions . . . they did it awkwardly, and then the other seemed to reprimand them.

Another skilful operation was performed by three older thieves, a carpenter, a French polisher, and a woman, all in their early or middle twenties. The woman first accosted their victim off the Haymarket while the others stood by. Then PC Murrell watched the three of them follow their prey down Panton and Oxendon Streets before Sarah Dean, the woman, stole his £10 watch from his coat and passed it down the line to each of her male companions.[32]

To the pickpocket the greatest boon was a crowd. We already noted

---

[31] Ibid., 1810, nos. 231, 370; 1820, no. 774; 1830, no. 932; 1840, no. 1426.

[32] Proceedings, 1810, nos. 331, 612; 1820, nos. 302, 344, 1083; 1850, no. 1098.

in our first two examples the role of the 'rowing match' that passed under Westminster Bridge in July 1810. Another victim, Joseph Lyon, a labourer, had his watch stolen when he was hustled by a crowd in Whitechapel one early evening in January 1810. The mayoral procession on Lord Mayor's Day (9 November) and the inaugural mayoral drive to the Guildhall at the end of the following January provided excellent opportunities for picking pockets; and Henry Norwood, a 16-year-old weaver, was seen robbing an unknown gentleman of his handkerchief as he walked 'among other suspected pickpockets mingling with a crowd in Strand and Chancery Lane waiting to see the Lord Mayor's carriage'. Further opportunities were provided by the elections held at the Guildhall to return the City's four Members to Parliament. In 1820 the elections lasted from 8 to 14 March. Three men were robbed of their handkerchiefs on 7, 10, and 14 March; but Edward Stanfield, a painter of Mortimer Street, Cavendish Square, did worse; for as he went to see his banker in Henrietta Street, Covent Garden, on the 13th—he remembered 'it was the time of the election' —he was pushed into the crowd by three young men, who stole his watch. The Middlesex election followed at Brentford Butts on 17 March; and here, too, there were pickings: Robert Balls, a grocer of Brentford, who 'attended Mr Whitbread to his carriage', was robbed of a £5 watch and his chain and seal. His thief, William Farmer, a bead-blower, who claimed he had gone to Brentford 'to meet my friends who are freeholders', was sentenced to transportation for life at the Old Bailey on 2 May of that year.

The most popular of the opposition candidates was Sir Francis Burdett, whose 'chairing' in the Haymarket and Knightsbridge on 4 and 6 April, after his re-election in Westminster, was the occasion of both celebration and the picking of pockets. Among the victims of these events were Isaac Queemby, a sheriff's officer from Northampton, who was robbed by two labourers of a pocket book and a £5 note; an unnamed sailor who lost a watch; and Robert Mayne, who worked in a floor-cloth manufactory in Kent Road and was attacked by twelve young men in the Haymarket; they stole from him a watch, two seals, and a key.[33]

But the greatest godsend of all to the pickpockets operating in the streets of Westminster and the City of London was the prolonged visit to the capital of Queen Caroline, the 'injured Queen' who had been

---

[33] *Proceedings*, 1820, nos. 354, 380, 388, 396–8, 430, 461, 474, 496, 564, 935.

rejected by her husband, George IV. Her cause was espoused by radical aldermen and a large part of the City's merchants and shop-keepers who fêted and adopted her rather as their forebears of half a century before had fêted and huzza-ed for John Wilkes. So when the Queen arrived from the Continent in early June 1820, she was greeted by an outburst of popular enthusiasm that continued intermittently until her death and funeral in London over a year later.[34] Inevitably, too, it was a period when the pickpocket came into his own.

On 6 June, the very day of the 'injured' Queen's return, Henry Cato, who was up in town for the day from Stafford, was robbed of a pocket book and a bill of exchange for £90 as he waited in Audley Street to see the Queen. On 3 July, Nicholas Dechemont, of Frith Street Soho, lost a £10 watch, two seals, and a ring as he waited in Oxford Street to watch the City professions return from presenting the Queen with an Address. On the 15th, John Marks lost a watch and chain as he stood in Pentonville and watched the Glass-blowers go by; a constable remarked: 'We afterwards took 14 more of the young men; Whiteworth and Chapman [two of Mark's assailants] were among them.' On the 24th, Joseph Fernie, an accountant of Leaden-hall Street, was stripped of his watch and seal as he watched the Weavers' Committee march along Bishopsgate Street with music and flags flying, and it was about this time that Samuel Furze also lost a watch as he saw the Queen climb into her carriage before a large crowd at her temporary residence (a mere 'cottage') in Portman Street.

One victim gave an interesting account of the pickpockets' be-haviour and composition at this time. He was John Middleton, a gentleman, who on 15 August, was robbed of a book, a purse, a watch and chain (£30), and seven £1 notes as he stood in the Strand watching the City procession on its way to present an Address to the Queen. He later told the court that his passage was barred by 'a crowd of persons along the Strand', twenty or more, who were 'what they called *ramping* [robbing] every gentleman who came along; they moved in a phalanx, keeping a little ahead of the Sheriff's carriage'. And he added: 'There were 25 or 26 of them, all young and generally genteelly dressed.'

Later in August, when Caroline moved into a more stately home in Brandenburg House, the crowds grew larger and the pickpockets more insistent. On the 22nd, James Stoner, a tailor of Skinner Street,

[34] See John Stevenson, 'The Queen Caroline Affair' in *London in the Age of Reform*, ed. J. Stevenson (Oxford, 1977), pp. 117–48.

was standing (as he thought) 'clear of the mob' in King Street, St James's Square; but he was robbed of his watch, a ribbon, and key (value £3. 10s. 2d.) by ten young men who dashed across the road to grab them. The next day, Richard Peters came from Duke Street, Lambeth, to see the Queen ride past the Horse Guards; he was robbed as he stood there of his watch and a seal (valued at £9 in all), by Peregrine Wood (it was said); yet, when arrested, the prisoner cried out indignantly: 'Me got your watch! Search me!' (Presumably they did and found no watch as he was acquitted at the Old Bailey soon after.) On the 24th, James Sherriff came up from Aylesbury, where he was Keeper of the Gaol, to watch the Queen pass through St James's Square; as a precaution he tucked his watch-seals under his waistcoat, but a seal and a chain were stolen all the same. On the 28th, Richard Chapman, a cabinet-maker of Ashley Street, was robbed of his watch, seals, and a ring as he stood opposite Caxton House, by two young men who were in the 'mob' around the Queen's carriage; and similar scenes were enacted on Westminster Bridge and in St James's the next day. On one of these occasions Constable Yates saw the prisoner, John Thompson, 'very active in the mob' and found six handkerchiefs on him after he 'attempted a dozen people's pockets'. Not surprisingly, he was sent to Australia for life. In another encounter a pocket book and a £5 note were taken from John Dean, of Swallow Street, as he stood in St James's Square while the Clerkenwell Address was being presented to the Queen; and, on 31 August, John Jones, a milkman of Tower Street, lost his watch and chain and two seals as he stood waiting to see the Queen drive down Parliament Street. It was a busy day for the police: an officer reported that 'about 40 thieves surrounded us; they attempted to take every gentleman's watch who came along'.

Further processions and Addresses followed during September and October, though at a slackened pace; and the activities of pickpockets are recorded in the Old Bailey *Proceedings* for 11, 13, and 25 September and 2 and 25 October. Another 'rowing match' also came to attract crowds to Tower Bridge, where a snuff box (20s.) was taken from William Smith, publican of the *Stone Kitchen* in the Tower. The constable of the Tower Ward reported: 'Just as the boats started, there was a sudden rush; I observed four or five bad characters...'[35]

After Queen Caroline's death and funeral procession in August

---

[35] *Proceedings*, 1820, nos. 396, 489, 625, 771–2, 925, 946, 1055, 1081–3, 1130, 1134, 1154, 1164, 1182, 1196, 1217–8, 1243, 1262, 1361.

1821 there followed an inevitably sharp decline in the exuberant Addresses of City merchants and the activities of the pickpockets that attended them. So there was quite a lull, but the succession of Queen Victoria in the late 1830s did not fail to draw the crowds again. We find examples for the following dates and occasions in 1840: the Queen's drive to the House of Lords on 16 January, when Peter Howard of Lambeth was robbed (of a mere handkerchief) in Parliament Street; a royal visit to the theatre in St James's, Piccadilly, on the evening of 28 February; and the 'night of Illuminations' on 25 May following Victoria's marriage to Albert. But it is perhaps worth recording that the heyday of pocket-picking was already past—partly due, maybe, to better policing, but probably more to the change in men's fashions which, by phasing out the 'fob' from the frontal waistline of breeches after 1829, left the gentleman's bejewelled watch—worn as much as an ornament as a time-keeper—less easily exposed to the attentions of the nimble thief: moreover, as the waistcoat lengthened in the 1830s, the watch began to be worn in a waistcoat pocket. So it is hardly a coincidence that, whereas in Queen Caroline's day the pick-pocket might get away with a £5, an £8 or a £10 watch, in the early Victorian age he would more likely have to settle for a cheap hand-kerchief, worth 2s. to 5s. 6d. at most, removed from the tail of a frock-coat or a long jacket (still persisting until 1850).[36]

[36] Proceedings, 1840, pp. 464–510 and nos. 550, 1040, 1590. See also, for changing fashions, C. Willett and Phillis Cunnington, Handbook of English Costume in the Eighteenth Century and Handbook of English Costume in the Nineteenth Century (Boston, 1969, 1970), passim.

3

CRITICAL

1. SUSSEX

THERE were about 2,000 prisoners tried at quarter sessions in Sussex in our five-year sample between 1805 and 1850 (1845 has been omitted for reasons explained before), and about half that number at assizes in our ten-year sample between 1810 and 1850. Of those tried at quarter sessions 88.9 per cent were male and 11.1 per cent were female, while at assizes the latter percentage fell to under 5. Moreover, about 70 per cent of all prisoners committed for trial were found guilty by the courts and, therefore, became 'criminal' by definition.[1] So if we are willing to accept that a 'criminal' is one who has been convicted at law, we must further conclude that the proportion of male 'criminals' to females was something in the order of 12 to 1. But was there such a thing as a distinctly female type of crime or criminal? This is a question we shall return to at the end of the chapter.

The more immediate question, however, is to which social group or class did the prisoner belong? It has, of course, been widely assumed—often without much further investigation—that prisoners or criminals in this early industrial age must overwhelmingly have come from the labouring or working classes. Nor does closer investigation altogether refute this assumption, but it brings refinements to the argument and helps us to give more precise answers to such questions as: what proportion were labourers? how many were skilled workers or crafts-men? how many, and in what proportions, do we find among such elements as shopkeepers, farmers, or even (of some evident importance in country districts) as gentlemen? And how do the answers to such questions vary between the counties? In Sussex (as in so many counties), the county court records are unfortunately not too precise in such matters, having the tendency to place all prisoners in three social groups and to label them as either 'gentlemen', 'yeomen', or 'labourers'. 'Gentlemen' and 'yeomen' (the latter nearly always

---

[1] Sussex QS Order Bks., 1805–50; Sussex Asizes, Agenda Bks. 21–32. For broadly similar ratios of Guilty to Not Guilty in Gloucestershire and London, see Glos. Pris. Regs. and OB *Proceedings*, 1805–50.

farmers and smallholders) are clear enough, but 'labourers' becomes an omnibus term to envelop the rest. In consequence, in Sussex the role of the labourer as a prisoner or criminal tends to become inflated and that of the craftsman or independent worker or self-employed to be played down.

So the following figures, based on information provided by the Order Books of the Sussex quarter sessions for the period 1805–50, while by no means useless, have to be taken with a pinch of salt.[2]

Labourers (including 'servants')	89.2 per cent
Skilled workers, craftsmen	2.7
Farmers ('yeomen')	1.0
Shopkeepers (tradesmen)	0.5
Gentlemen	0.6
Wives, widows, etc. not already included under 'labourers'	6.0
	100.0

If we now turn to our 10-yearly sample based on the Agenda Books of the Sussex assizes, another disappointment awaits us: there are no occupations, indeed no 'social' labels whatever, provided for 1810 and 1820, so that any comparison will have to be limited to the years 1830, 1840, and 1850. If we now set these two sets of figures together, we shall find (as we should expect) a smaller proportion of craftsmen and a significantly higher proportion of labourers, while gentlemen, shopkeepers, and farmers are so insignificant as not to be shown at all (see Table 3.1).

Table 3.1. *Social categories of Sussex prisoners, 1830–1850**

	(a) Quarter Sessions			(b) Assizes		
	1830	1840	1850	1830	1840	1850
Labourers	72.0	84.3	88.0	61.6	55.0	52.0
Craftsmen	0.5	–	–	15.9	12.0	13.0
Shopkeepers	2.0	–	–	–	–	–
Farmers	4.0	–	–	–	–	–
Gentlemen	1.4	1.2	–	–	–	–

* Shown as a percentage of all categories listed. See note 1.

2 Coll. W&M CC; calculations based on Sussex QS Order Bks. 1805–50.

In the case of the records at quarter sessions, we may go further by looking more closely at not only broad social groups but at the occupations that occur most frequently against the names of the accused. In addition to the labourers and servants (working on farms, in shops, and in domestic service), the occupations most frequently listed are the following, placed here in descending order of magnitude as a percentage of the whole (it must be remembered that, after the deduction of the 89.2 per cent for labourers and servants, there only remained a meagre 10.8 per cent to distribute among the rest!):

Brickmakers	0.78
Brewers	0.36
Carpenters	0.31
Weavers	0.31
Grocers	0.26
Soldiers and Sailors	0.21
Silver polishers	0.21
Trunkmakers	0.16
Toll collectors	0.16

If we now take account, in addition, of a number of other occupations (so infrequently occurring as not considered worthy of listing here), we may attempt to draw up a number of broader occupational categories that may reveal the *sort* of workers that most frequently contributed to crime in Sussex at this time. We shall then find that the *building trades* (with brickmakers, bricklayers, painters, paviors, and plasterers) probably make up the largest group with a proportion of a little over 2 per cent. There follow *food and drink* (grocers, brewers, fishmongers, butchers) with about 0.8 per cent; and other *service* or *consumer trades* (blacksmiths, wheelwrights, tailors, shoemakers, polishers, grooms, and shopworkers) that contribute another 0.75. So very little remains for the more specifically *industrial* trades, which can only muster in this list a single railwayman, 6 weavers, and 2 stockmakers, accounting at most for 0.6 per cent of the whole.[3] But Gloucestershire, as we shall see, will produce a very different picture.

Finally, in this section, let us look again from the general to the particular, from the statistics and percentages to the individual case-studies. Let us see for a while how some of these labourers, craftsmen, shopkeepers, farmers, and gentry behaved and, in consequence of this

---

[3] See note 1.

behaviour, came to be included among all these statistical data in the
first place.

As the cases selected involve conflict, either within a given social
group or in association with another, or again in opposition to another
group whose interests appear hostile to its own, they all involve
assault. So let us start with the strange case of William Henry
Bacchus Esq., a gentleman of Wivelsfield in East Sussex. For reasons
that the records do not reveal, Bacchus collected a mixed group—an
auctioneer, a roadman, and a labourer appear with him among those
indicted at the next sessions—to teach his wife Eliza a lesson. So they
assaulted her, and beat and wounded her, for which the court found
them guilty (except the labourer, who may have got involved against
his will) and fined Bacchus, as the principal assailant, £5, and the
auctioneer and the roadman 5s. each.

Another assault case involved farmers and labourers on opposing
sides in a confrontation that had evident class undertones. On 23
August 1829, at East Dean, in West Sussex, Hugh Penfold the
Younger, yeoman of the parish of Wiggonholt, together with James
Penfold, his brother, and Charles Collick, a chemist of East Dean,
and two other farmers of the district, assaulted and wounded John
Biddle, a labourer, also of East Dean. The court dismissed the charges
against James Penfold and Collick, but fined the three others, including the principal defendant, £30. But why did Hugh Penfold behave
in this way?; and why did he bring together fellow-farmers and
others to support him in an assault that took some of them (like
John Olliver of Annering) several miles from their village to the scene
of the affray? We do not know and the report of the case gives us no
direct answer; but, indirectly, we know at least that other labourers
rallied to defend the victim and helped him get his own back on his
assailants. For, the same day, two later cases tell us, the same Hugh
Penfold the Younger was in turn assaulted and beaten badly by a
number of labourers that included the original victim, John Biddle,
and three others, all labourers of Petworth (it is significant that they,
at least, having only their own legs to carry them, all came from the
same village). It is also no doubt significant that the court, while it
fined three of the original aggressors £30 each, acquitted the four
labourers, deeming perhaps that, whatever had provoked the conflict,
it had by now become a simple matter of tit for tat.[4]

<hr>

4 Ibid.

On 5 November 1834 there was another case of collective action by men of the 'middling sort'; but this time tradesmen not farmers—a baker, a tailor, and two carpenters, all living at Petworth. It was a case of riotous assembly in the same town and of an assault on three peace officers, Samuel Greenfield and Edmund Joiner, constables of the tything of Rotherbridge, and Robert Haslett, tything man of Petworth. So it was clearly a dispute over tithe—an issue that had arisen sharply, along with a number of other issues, in the labourers' movement of 1830 and which in several counties (including Sussex) had sometimes brought farmers and labourers together in common protest against landlords and parsons.

In some other collective actions it was the labourers that took the lead, as in the assault on William Parker, peace officer at Cuckfield, on 18 September 1834. The purpose of the assault was evidently to release prisoners, for the record of the case describes the action as 'thereby preventing the lawful apprehension of G. Brigden and Henry Jennings for stealing 3 gold sovereigns and 5 half-sovereigns, 4 silver half-crowns and 30 silver shillings—£7. 10s. in all—the property of Patrick Max Cann [sic!]', a resident of Cuckfield.

Similarly, certain inhabitants and freeholders of East Grinstead acted collectively when they chose to save their money and labour rather than repair (as they were obliged to do) 'a certain common, a part of the King's Highway within the parish of East G–d, i.e. a turnpike–rd leading from the Town of Croydon [Surrey] to East G–, ending at Hazleden (?)'. When brought to court by an indignant fellow-inhabitant, the malingerers pleaded guilty to a charge of neglect and were fined, not ungenerously, the sum of 1s. a head.[6]

2. GLOUCESTERSHIRE

There were about 3,900 prisoners tried in Gloucestershire within our five-year sample between 1815 and 1850; of these around 2,200 were tried at quarter sessions and 1,700 at assizes. The proportion of women to men was a little higher than in Sussex, with 87.5 per cent males and 12.5 per cent females for quarter sessions and assizes combined, whereas in Sussex (as we saw) the proportions in quarter sessions were

[5] Ibid., 1835.
[6] Ibid., 1830.

fairly similar: 88.9 to 11.9; though, at assizes, the percentages of women prisoners fell to 5 per cent or less.[7]

In the prison registers for Gloucestershire we meet with none of the frustrations we experienced in the records of both courts in Sussex. The occupations are clearly stated so that we can obtain a reasonably accurate picture of the numbers and proportions of labourers and craftsmen among the prisoners brought to trial, as well as of the gentry, farmers, and shopkeepers, and other social groups. Moreover, we are provided with such information about prisoners as their age, their degree of literacy, and their village of origin, as well as the village where the crime was committed. So we have the following facts about prisoners for which there is no equivalent in Sussex, or for that matter in most other county records.

Ages. Of the 3,900 prisoners held in our five-year sample, 1.3 per cent were under 13 years of age, 29.24 were aged 13 to 19, 29.2 per cent between 20 and 29, 19.75 per cent between 30 and 45, 5.75 per cent between 46 and 59, and 2.2 per cent aged 60 and above, leaving 1.9 per cent as 'unknowns'. So there are no real surprises, with 1.3 per cent juvenile, 5.75 per cent middle-aged, and 2.2 per cent aged, leaving the bulk of the able-bodied to be divided into three main age-groups: 29.2 per cent in their teens, 39.9 per cent in their twenties, and 19.75 per cent in their thirties to mid-forties.[8]

Literacy. Of 3,100 prisoners, 27.83 per cent could *read*, 40.46 could *read and write*, and 30.71 per cent could do *neither*. So, for practical purposes, we should apply the term 'literate' only to the 40.46 that could both read and write.[9]

Mobility. Of 3,060 prisoners from our sample, more committed crimes outside their own village than within it, the proportions being 51.55 per cent in the first case and 48.45 per cent in the second, and the

[7] Glos. Pris. Regs. 1815–50; Coll. W&M CC.

[8] Women pprisoners tended to be younger than the men: of a total of 457 whose ages are recorded (leaving only 13 'unknowns'), 33.19 per cent were in their teens 38.30 per cent in their 20s, and 16.38 per cent in their 30s to mid-40s (Glos. Pris. Regs. 1815–50; Coll. W&M CC).

[9] Not surprisingly, women prisoners were less literate than the men: of 2,697 men and 398 women, 24.99 per cent of the men could *only read* and 27.89 per cent of the women; and 42.27 per cent men could *read and write* (or could, broadly speaking, claim to be literate) but only 27.89 per cent of the women. Yet — and this perhaps reflects the inadequacy of the literacy test — 32.74 per cent of the men could *neither read nor write* compared with only 24.87 per cent of the women (Ibid.).

percentages of women prisoners committing crimes outside their village was slightly higher. Taking account of poor roads and the paucity of communications at this time, these figures suggest a surprising degree of mobility among the county's rural population.[10]

We return to our direct comparison with Sussex by exploring once more the social and occupational composition of the prisoners. Compared with Sussex, as we should expect, there is a slight fall in the number of labourers; yet it is not startling. To begin with the men and women tried at quarter sessions. Of these, 93.3 per cent are termed labourers in 1815 (but the sample—16—is too small to be given credibility), 80.4 per cent in 1820 (the first complete sessions year), 87.8 in 1825, 87.7 in 1831, 90 per cent in 1840 (quarter sessions and assizes combined), 91.1 per cent in 1845, and 88.2 per cent in 1850. In the records of assizes the proportion of labourers is almost the same, maintaining from 1820 to 1850 a steady level of 83 to 90 per cent and only diverging significantly from this level during the few months included for 1815, when the assizes figure of 57.1 per cent (based on a sample of 14 labourers) can be considered no more reliable than the figure of 93.3 that emerged from the sessions.

In the case of craftsmen and other social groups there is no appreciable difference between the two Gloucester courts, whereas between Sussex and Gloucester there are significant differences in respect of the other social groups, which, in the case of craftsmen and gentry, are startling. The point may be best illustrated by setting the combined figures for each category of the two Gloucester courts side by side with the Sussex totals based on the quarter sessions we have already noted in our previous section (see Table 3.2).

And now, as we did for Sussex, let us look more closely at the occupations of individual prisoners and at the broader occupational categories to which they may be said to belong. In this case, as has been already explained, we have more reliable information about the occupations of prisoners, but only for two consecutive years in our five-year sample, for 1835 and 1840. By adding the two years' totals together we have a combined figure of 890 cases spread over 102 occupations. As labourers and servants on the list account for a little over 61 per cent of the prisoners, we are left with a little under 39 per cent to take care of the rest. However, for practical purposes, it has

---

10 Of 385 women recorded, 52.99 per cent committed crimes outside their village and 47.01 per cent within it (ibid.).

Table 3.2. Social categories of prisoners in (a) Gloucester (b) Sussex*

| | Gloucester | | | | | | | | Sussex |
	1815	1820	1825	1831	1835	1840	1845	1850	1805–50 (incl.)
Labourers	69.8	83.2	85.6	88.2	88.0	77.4	88.1	86.9	89.2
Skilled	13.9	6.3	9.9	6.1	6.5	6.7	4.6	3.2	2.7
Farmers	2.3	0.3	–	0.2	0.2	0.2	0.7	1.2	1.0
Shopkeepers	2.3	2.1	–	1.2	0.6	0.6	0.7	0.9	0.5
Gentlemen	–	–	–	–	–	–	–	–	0.6
Women	–	–	–	–	4.0	6.25	–	–	6.0(?)

* Percentages of total number of prisoners. Glos. Pris. Regs. 1815–50; Sussex QS Order Bks., 1805–50; Coll. W&M CC.

been thought best to limit the remaining 100 occupations to the 22 that attain a minimal rating of 0.5 per cent per head. The following picture then emerges:[11]

Occupation	% Indictments	Occupation	% Indictments
Shoemakers	3.0	Soldiers and sailors	.90
Weavers	3.0	Carpenters	.90
Clothworkers/dressers	2.4	Stonemasons	.90
Tailors	1.9	Chimneysweeps	.90
Bakers	1.7	Spinners	.80
Coalminers	1.3	Hatters	.80
Blacksmiths	1.2	Trampers (tramps)	.80
Sawyers	1.2	Dressmakers	.70
Butchers	1.15	Hawkers	.56
Gardeners	1.1	Grooms	.56
Watermen	1.0	Basketmakers	.56

If we now once more turn to the broader occupational categories, we may reallocate these occupations roughly as follows (in the customary descending order of magnitude):

1. *Service* and *consumer* trades (blacksmiths, chimneysweeps, dressmakers, gardeners, grooms, shoemakers, tailors)   10.35 per cent
2. *Industrial* trades (basketmakers, clothworkers, coalminers, factory workers [only 1], spinners, weavers)   8.1 per cent

11 Glos. Pris. Regs. 1815–50; W&M CC.

3. *Building* trades (carpenters, sawyers, stonemasons) 3.0 per cent
4. *Food* and *drink* (butchers, bakers) 2.85 per cent

So, even if this picture is not as complete as we might wish—accounting for only one-third to one-quarter of the county's crime according to our five-year sample—it clearly shows that the industrial workers in Gloucester—miners, weavers, and clothworkers in particular—unlike their counterparts in Sussex, had already begun to make a substantial contribution to the proportion of crimes committed.

Evidently, this contribution was already apparent long before the period covered by the two years on which we have drawn so far. To illustrate the point let us take some examples of criminal activity by industrial workers from the quarter sessions and assizes of 1825 and 1831. First from the Epiphany sessions of January 1825, where two such cases were heard: that against John Wood, 17, a shearer, who was charged with stealing a leaden weight from a shearing machine in Thomas Shurmer's workshop at Horsley; and that in which Henry Critchley, a 26-year-old machine worker of Longford, was charged with stealing a watch from James Millard, a clothworker of Bisley, near Stroud, on 4 November 1824.

Three other cases belong to the Lent Assizes held in March of that year. There was John Berriman, 19, a cloth dresser of Chalford, who broke into Thomas Smart's shop and stole a variety of goods. Another cloth dresser, James Churches (*alias* Jeffreyes), 25, of Painswick, in the night of 27 November 1824 broke into the house of Nathaniel Churches (a father, an uncle, or a cousin, perhaps) and stole an assortment of food and valuables. The third case involved Henry Perrett, 20, a clothier of North Nibley, who broke into the warehouse of Daniel and Nathaniel Lloyd, clothiers of Uley, in November 1824 and stole some pieces of cloth.

Finally, we may cite three further cases of the kind of which two were heard at the Lent Assizes of 1831 and one at the Trinity sessions of 1835. The first two involved clothing workers: in one case, John Ashmead, 16, of Nailsworth, who stole a coat from George William Saunders at Avening; and in the second, Esmé Window, 15, who stole silver from Samuel Francis's house at Stroud. In the third case, a clothing worker and two cloth dressers were found guilty of stealing four pieces of cashmere cloth and a piece of broad cloth from Messrs Obediah Paul Within and Henry Cecil, clothiers of Woodchester. Two

men were transported for seven years and the third, having turned
King's Evidence, was discharged.[12]

3. LONDON

A little over 4,500 prisoners were tried at the Middlesex Assizes
within our ten-year sample between 1810 and 1850. These included an
appreciably higher proportion of women than we found at either
assizes or quarter sessions in Sussex or Gloucester. To spell out the
figures one year at a time: 23 per cent of those tried at the Old
Bailey in 1810 were women, 16.8 per cent in 1820, 21.2 in 1830, 21.7
in 1840, and 18.2 per cent in 1850, with an overall percentage for
the half-century of 22.3. The proportion of women taken into custody
by the Metropolitan Police between 1831 and 1850 was considerably
higher, being 35.7 per cent in 1832, 33 per cent in 1840, and 33.5 per
cent in 1850; but it fell back to 25 per cent of those committed for
trial.[13]

The proportion of labourers and servants, on the other hand, was
far lower than in the rural counties, presumably because of the almost
total absence of farms. For 1810 I have counted only 32.5 per cent for
labourers, but rising to 54.5 per cent in 1820, 65.5 in 1830, 67 per cent
in 1840, and 63.5 per cent in 1850. Craftsmen, however, played a
larger part, as we should expect, as did shopkeepers, clerks, and professionals, and also 'unknowns' (see note to Table 3.4), while farmers
and gentry had dropped out altogether. Table 3.3 takes account of all
the major social categories of prisoners brought to trial at the Old
Bailey betwen 1810 and 1850 and gives us a bird's eye view of the
whole affair.

[12] Glos. Pris. Regs. 1825, 1831, 1835. As a prelude to discussing female crime
and criminality, we may add four more cases of larceny by women clothing
workers from 1845 and 1850. In July 1845, Leah Walton, 12, who worked in a
silk factory, was charged with stealing clothes from the Guardians of the Union
at Shipton in Stow; and Mary Ann Hillman, a 'factory girl', was charged with
stealing a linen cape at Stroud in the same month. In October 1850, also at
Stroud, Dinah Smart, a 'factory spinner', was charged with stealing a loaf of
bread and an umbrella; and, in December, Martha Bisp, a shirtmaker of Winter-
bourne, who was paid at the rate of 9d. a shirt, was charged with stealing a
box worth £1. 13s. 7½d. Hillman and Bisp were acquitted and Walton and
Smart were sentenced to short terms in jail (Glos. Pris. Regs., Summer Assizes,
1845; Michaelmas and Epiphany QS, 1850.)
[13] OB *Proceedings*, 1810–1850; MPC R., 1832–50.

Table 3.3. *Prisoners at London Assizes 1810–1850 in main social groups as percentages of all indictments**

Social Group	1810	1820	1830	1840	1850
Labourers and servants	32.5	54.5	65.5	67.0	63.5
Craftsmen	2.5	5.0	2.1	2.5	1.8
Shopkeepers, petty tradesmen	1.9	4.3	4.0	3.7	7.5
Clerks	–	–	0.7	1.1	3.0
Soldiers, sailors	2.6	5.1	2.4	3.0	–
Women†	23.9	16.8	21.2	21.7	18.2
Miscellaneous	1.1	3.8	2.1	–	4.0
Unknown	35.5	10.5	2.0	1.0	2.0
	100.0	100.0	100.0	100.0	100.0

* OB *Proceedings*, 1810–50; London RO, Newgate Calendars, 1820–50 (OB/CB, registers, vols. 4, 9, 17, 18).

† For the wider problems involved in female criminality see the last pages of this chapter.

I have divided the Old Bailey prisoners in my sample for 1810 to 1850 into 174 occupations. Of these the following 40 are the most significant with 10 appearances or more in the court of the Old Bailey during these years (once more in descending order of magnitude):

Occupations	Indictments	Occupations	Indictments
Labourers, servants	1,180	Cabinet-makers	26
Wives, widows, spinsters	538	Hatters	26
Shoemakers	131	Hawkers	26
Sailors, mariners	93	Printers	20
Prostitutes	81	Watermen, boatmen	19
Tailors	62	Drapers	18
Carpenters	53	Plasterers	18
Clerks	51	Errand boys	16
Grooms, stablemen	48	Jewellers	16
Painters	43	Fruiterers	15
Bakers	41	Gardeners	15
Weavers	40	Barbers	14
Bricklayers	39	Barmen	14
Butchers	35	Bookbinders	13
Porters	35	Watch and clockmakers	13
Smiths	35	Grocers	12

Occupations	Indictments	Occupations	Indictments
Soldiers	31	French polishers	11
Dealers, merchants	31	Sawyers	11
Boys (under 15)	29	Carters	10
Chimney sweeps	29	Occupation unknown	1,244
Coachmen, carmen	28		

If we now follow a similar procedure to the one we used before and place these occupations in broader occupational groups, we may arrive at the picture presented in Table 3.4.

Table 3.4

Occupational groups	No. indictments	% all indictments
Labourers (inc. 72 servants)	1,108	26.8
Women (not included in other groups)	538	13.0
Building trades: bricklayers, carpenters, cabinet-makers, painters, plasterers, plumbers, sawyers, stonemasons	203	4.9
Consumer trades: inc. food, drink, barbers, sweeps	171	4.1
Clothing: drapers, hatters, shoemakers, spinners, tailors, 20 weavers	167	4.0
Domestic service: incl. 14 coachmen, gardeners, 24 grooms, porters, 71 servants	160	3.9
Luxury trades: bookbinders, booksellers, goldsmiths, jewellers, prostitutes, watch and clockmakers	157	3.8
Foreign trade: sailors, mariners	93	2.2
'Industrial': 35 smiths, 20 weavers, brass founders, braziers, turners, a dozen small crafts, 3 clothing workers	90	2.2
Inland transport: bargemen, 14 coachmen, 24 grooms, saddlers, harness makers, watermen, only 1 railwayman (a porter)	79	1.9
Banking, business: clerks, errand boys	67	1.6
Petty commerce: dealers, hawkers	57	1.4
Occupations unknown:*	1,244	30.1

* The large numbers of 'unknowns' are largely due to the absence of Newgate Calendars for 1810 and gaps in 1820.

This is clearly a very different picture from the one we saw in the two rural counties. The number of labourers has further shrunk, not only to allow for the virtual absence of farm workers (there were two shepherds in all), so common in both Sussex and Gloucester, but also due to the considerable spread of unskilled workers over other occupations as well (we have transferred, for example, half the 'servants' to the separate category of domestic service). Again, as in Sussex though not in Gloucester, industrial workers come pretty low on the list: in this case after building, consumer trades, clothing, domestic service, and both luxury and foreign trade. Moreover, the industrial occupations appearing among the Old Bailey indictments are mainly few and far between. There are no coalminers (as we should expect) and only one railwayman and three clothing workers; 20 weavers have been included and 35 smiths, though these may well be an exaggeration; and a score of braziers, founders, turners, and others of the petty productive crafts who may, or may not, have been employed in industrial production, as the miners and clothiers of the county of Gloucester undoubtedly were.[14]

Once more we return to the particular cases in the hope of finding some answers to the question: what sort of Londoners committed crimes or were indicted to answer charges at the Old Bailey assizes? A few prisoners achieved notoriety or fame, including two men whose names appear in consecutive months in the Proceedings for 1820. One was Arthur Thistlewood, the Cato Street conspirator, whose trial, along with that of his eleven companions, began at the Court of Justice in April 1820, lasted for sixty-five days and took up sixty-two pages of the printed Proceedings. These men were charged, with the aid of a Government informer who had entered their ranks, with conspiring to blow up Lord Liverpool's cabinet. Thistlewood and five others were hanged, their heads severed and their bodies left to hang in chains—the last survival of a barbarous medieval custom—and a further five were transported to Australia, where the youngest man, John Strange, rose to become Chief Constable at Bathurst, in New South Wales, and was pardoned after serving twenty-two years of exile.[15]

The other prisoner, whose life is recorded in the Australian Dictionary of Biography, was the Danish adventurer, Jørgen Jørgenson, who early in his career, when enlisted on the British side

14 An obvious omission is dock labour, which receives no specific mention in the trial reports. We must assume that dockworkers are included among 'labourers' and also among the numerous crafts that are spread widely, though thinly, over my list.

15 OB Proceedings, 1820, pp. 215–77; G. Rudé, Protest and Punishment, pp. 194–5.

in the Anglo-Dutch war against Napoleon, sailed to Iceland in command of a privateer, arrested the Danish governor, and proclaimed the island's independence with himself as Head of State, a position that he held for a bare nine weeks. His adventures in the next twelve years had no such glamour, ending in his arrest in London in May 1820 for a larceny in Sarah Stourbridge's lodging house in Warren Street, Fitzroy Square. The lodger, who had boasted of being a 'gentleman' and of his friendship with Lord Castlereagh, one night decamped carrying with him his bed (40s.), a bolster (5s.), two blankets (4s.), and a quilt (2s.) which he pledged with a pawnbroker along the Tottenham Court Road. He was sentenced to transportation for seven years; but, after a number of visits to Newgate, he only arrived in Australia, now with a life sentence, in 1826. He settled in Van Diemen's Land (today's Tasmania), became a constable and an explorer, secured a pardon and wrote histories and travelogues; but he remained the immoderate drinker that he had always been and, in January 1841, died at Hobart of 'inflammation of the lungs'.[16]

We should perhaps also add a third prisoner of some notoriety, who in 1850 appeared for trial at the Old Bailey where he was charged with an attempt to assassinate the Queen. He was Robert Pate, of 27 Duke Street, a 'well dressed' gentleman and former officer in the 10th Hussars. Slightly crazy, he had already accused his cook of trying to poison him. On this occasion, he appears to have felt slighted— perhaps in relation to his pension?— and sought revenge, or redress, by swishing his cane at the Queen as she drove in Royal procession through St James's. It was a trivial gesture, but it caused alarm; and Pate was transported to Australia for a seven-year term. Unlike Jørgenson, his name is not recorded in the *Australian Dictionary of Biography*.[17]

None of the other prisoners in our sample made as great an impression as these three; but some of them attract our attention for a variety of qualities, both good and bad, that they displayed in court or when arrested by the police and brought to Bow Street. Some for their cheek, their ready repartee, or willingness to argue or answer back. John Porter, a 21-year-old labourer, for example, who, when arrested for stealing 3¾ yards of silk (worth 40s.) from Alexander Bidwood, thought it 'a hard thing to be imprisoned for nothing'; and James Swayne, sentenced to be transported for seven years for stealing

16 OB *Proceedings*, 1820, no. 701; ADB, II, 1788–1850, 26–8.
17 OB *Proceedings*, 1850, no. 1300.

6 lb. lead (1s.) and a brass cock from a building, found it hard to accept the verdict: 'It is a d–d hard thing you can't let a man get his living.' Michael Roach, a young tailor, who had stolen two coats (£3) and twelve pairs of trousers from a dwelling house and was told he would be transported for 15 years as he had been previously convicted of a felony, objected: 'but that is no reason why I should be guilty of this'. John Patterson, an elderly tailor (he was 65) passed a customer a bad shilling to pay for a couple of herrings, and offered another to the customer's wife. He gave a curious explanation for his conduct: 'From my great age [he said] I am liable to be imposed on by my customers.' The court was not impressed and sent him to jail for twelve months. One prisoner, sentenced to transportation for having stolen 17 lb. buck leather (25s.) from a shoemaker in Lisson Grove, not only gave an alibi (which was not accepted) but stated 'he was in the New Police when he was taken' (this was in November 1829, soon after the new force had been set up). George Humphries, who walked into a linen draper's shop in Henrietta Street, Covent Garden, was charged with stealing 32 yards of the best blue woollen cloth, worth £32; he objected to the terms of the charge: 'The cloth has grown', he protested in court, 'it has got four yards bigger since I came from Bow Street.' The charge of burglary brought against the prisoner was changed to one of larceny as he had evidently not broken into the shop; but he was sentenced to death all the same and reproved in addition for his 'very impertinent' remarks.[18]

Other prisoners quite stoically accepted their fate or even welcomed a sentence of transportation. William Patterson Flanaghan, a 36-year-old printer who was sentenced to be transported for seven years for stealing a powder flask (6s.), three caps, a seal-skin cap, a quilt, and a blanket (22s.) from a public house, welcomed the verdict and insisted that he 'sought for transportation'—possibly because he had fallen on hard times: he told the court that in his former job as a printer he had earned 104 gns. a year. There was also Andrew Daniels, 27, a labourer who, in June 1850, was sentenced to a second term of transportation (the first was imposed in December 1845) for stealing a silver watch (£4) from Mary Ann Gathercole, of Eccleston Place, Pimlico. On being arrested, he is reputed to have told the police: 'I stole it and sold it [to Moses Samuels, a receiver], and hope I shall be transported for it.' It was a hope he shared with many an Irish labourer at this time, in the

---

[18] *Proceedings*, 1820, nos. 310, 469; 1840, no. 666; 1850, no. 164.

hideous aftermath of the great Irish Famine of '45. Another person who accepted his fate was William Cox, a mariner, who had been caught removing 50 lb. of lead from the roof of a warehouse in Stepney. When the owner, a general merchant, challenged him with the words: 'I have got you at last. I have been looking for you for a long time, for the people have been robbed four or five times', he replied quite simply: 'I suppose I must pay for all' (he, too, was transported to Australia for seven years).[19]

Some prisoners were scrupulously polite in dealing with their victims, showed due contrition in court or, despite their recent fall from grace, enjoyed a generally good reputation among their victims or employers. John William German, a bootmaker, wrote to his victim, Jesse Clarkson, a hairdresser of Wandsworth, after he had robbed him of four tea-cloths, worth 22s.: 'You will no doubt feel shocked to find I have been your enemy instead of your friend; my respects to the cook.' Charles Evans, an errand boy, who had stolen from his employer, James Swallow, a purse, a ring, and 3 gns. from his house-keeper, told the court that sentenced him: 'I humbly beg leave to state that when I engaged in this transaction I had no idea of the extent of criminality attached to it'; and he assured the court of his 'sincere contrition'. And James Webber, 20, who had been Samuel Scott's servant for 12 months before he burgled his house for 49 silver spoons (£20), heard his employer tell the court that 'he never found the prisoner dishonest and had trusted him with all he had'. The defendant was sentenced to death; but he was recommended to mercy on the grounds of his good character and the belief that he had been 'misled by evil men'.[20]

Among the women, prostitutes appear to have stood out as the champions of what they believed to be their rights. Mary Revlet, a widow described as a 'woman of the Town', who lodged in Newton Court, Wild Street, in Covent Garden, was charged with stealing four £1 notes from the person of George Edwards, a coal dealer of Chandos Street. But she refused to give back more than half the money, as 'she had earned her £2 and would not give it up'. (The case was dismissed; but, two months later, the same Mary Revlet, now rather incongruously known as 'modest Mary', robbed a man of a £4 watch and—once more—of four £1 notes in a public house in Bedfordbury, also in Covent

[19] Proceedings, 1820, no. 913; 1830, no. 506; 1840, no. 1656.

[20] Proceedings, 1820, nos. 468, 821; 1830, no. 452; 1840, nos. 596, 1894; 1850, no. 1272.

Garden; but this time she was transported for 7 years.) Eliza Bryson, who was charged with stealing 8s. from Evan Roberts in a courtyard in Sun Street, Bishopsgate, was inspired by a similar sense of justice. When the plaintiff only offered her 6d., she took the 8s. from his waistcoat pocket and gave him 4s. back. 'She deserved the money', said a witness. And Margaret Hull, another prostitute (or 'unfortunate girl'), entertained Richard Reeder, a smith, in her upstairs room in Vinegar Lane, St George's, where, it was alleged, she robbed him of his watch and chain. With some warmth she told the constable sent to arrest her that she would return the watch only if her victim agreed to pay her 5s. for the use of her room. But, of course, this excuse did not always work: when Catharine Madigan, in October 1840, robbed a client of a £2. 17s. watch on the grounds that he had only paid her a shilling, she was transported for ten years to Australia.

Sometimes women took the lead in a criminal enterprise, as when Mary Wood (18) and Jim Regan (15) robbed John Brigg's six-year-old daughter of 4s. 6d., the change from the 5s. piece that her father had given her to buy a loaf of bread. As the two robbers ran away from the scene of their crime, it was Wood who was heard to give her companion the warning: 'Don't split or we shall be booked.' In another case involving larceny, Susan Haris (16) stole 6 lb. of bacon worth 4s. from a cheesemonger's shop in Fitzroy Square. She had two accomplices, William Jones (15) and William Harrison (14); but at their trial George Anthony, a witness, told the court: 'I had every reason to believe that the boys are the dupes of the female prisoner; I have seen her about.' His judgement was accepted; and while the two boys escaped with nine days' jail and a whipping, the girl was sent to prison for three full months.[21]

Some prisoners, far from being courteous, good-tempered, or amusing, were bloody-minded and violent in both their words and behaviour. Joseph Skelton, an irascible dustman, was charged with murder when he lost his temper in a crowded thoroughfare in Covent Garden. His dust-cart was held up by a coalheaver in Chandos Street; so, wild with fury, he drove his horse onto the pavement, crushing his victim who died soon after. (This time the prisoner was luckier than he deserved and got off with a verdict of manslaughter and a year in jail.) When Richard Connors and his wife Mary stole two gowns (10s.) and other goods from Mary Anderson, a fellow-

[21] *Proceedings*, 1810, nos. 110, 250, 341, 654; 1820, no. 1280; 1840, no. 2602; 1850, no. 110.

lodger in Josephine Iredale's dwelling house, it was said that the two defendants, to compel their victim to co-operate, 'terrorized' her without mercy, a process that is graphically described in the Old Bailey account. Another victim of violence was Thomas Tollman, of Hampton, on the outskirts of London, who, having fastened his locks and retired to bed early, was rudely awakened past midnight by three soldiers of the 21st Regiment who broke in, demanded money, and took away £5, having first tied a cord round their victim's neck to attempt to get more. Sarah Smith, who had lived with George Argent, a wine porter of Whitechapel, for eight or nine years, returned to the house after three weeks' separation and threw vitriol in his face so that he lost the sight of one eye. Thomas Howard, a 30-year-old carpenter, displayed his violence in both words and deeds when he assaulted and wounded PC B 210 to prevent his arrest. He threatened all 'bloody buggers' who got in his way with a knife, swore to the victim 'I'll suck your blood and drain every drop out of you', and left him disabled for eleven days. Alexander Lovell, who stole three straw hats (40s.) from Catharine Wallis's shop in Holborn, uttered similar blood-curdling threats to his woman victim: 'B–t you, I'll stick a knife in your b–y guts!' And when William Murray and John Crawley, a sailor, broke into John Henry's house at 3 Little Bell Court, Gray's Inn Lane, in the early morning of 20 March 1810 and stole two curtains and a tea-tray (3s.), Crawley threatened Sarah Todd, the lodger, in the following uncomplimentary terms: 'You b–y whore, if you make a noise, I will cut your throat!'[22]

Even nastier were the cases of blackmail accompanied by threats to expose alleged acts of sexual deviation. In one such case, the prisoner, William Cane, a deserter from the Regiment of Guards, assaulted William Price, a purveyor to the Army Medical Board, and stole his watch, worth £5. 7s., threatening if he demurred to expose him for sodomy. A week later, he blackmailed him for a further £5 and followed this up with a demand for £50 and then £100. Yet he was taken to court and there, for good measure, accused his victim of making a sexual assault on him. The blackmail failed and the accuser, become defendant, was sentenced to death for assault and robbery. A similar case involved William Wilkinson, who assaulted Edward Hodder in the parish of St George and robbed him of 7s. 6d. in cash and two £1 notes, threatening his victim with a charge of the

22 *Proceedings*, 1810, no. 604; 1820, no. 628.

'unnatural crime' of sodomy. 'The particulars', added the court chronicler demurely, 'are of too indelicate a nature for publication.'[23]

Occasionally in these records we come near to a criminal under-world, but, even at the end of our period, the case was still rather rare. John Glynn, a 24-year-old labourer, was charged with 'receiving' 3 lb. of soap (1s.), the property of Daniel Cooper, a cornchandler of Eyre Street Hill, off Field Lane, which had originally been stolen by three boys who had sold it to the prisoner for 5d. The incident seems insignificant enough, involving a quite derisory sum; but Constable G 127 told the court that the prisoner 'belonged to a notorious gang of thieves and had been several times previously convicted', and he was transported for ten years for what on the face of it seemed a trivial offence. Another case, which involved the burglary of the dwelling house of Israel Joseph, a watchmaker of Drury Lane, by four women and a man who stole 25 watches, 75 pencil cases, and 20 seals (a £49 haul in all), was an 'inside' job, as one of the prisoners, Mrs Ann Mason, lodged in the house and it appears that the bureau had been left open. An interesting feature of the story is the suggested part in the exploit played by a Mr Schooley, a professional lock-picker and safe-cracker. The real smell of a criminal *milieu* penetrates even more strongly in the strange case of John Nash and John Hurley of Rosemary Lane, charged with taking £22. 4s. from the poor boxes at St Bartholomew's Hospital in West Smithfield. Both men had been previously convicted and Nash had planned the recent operation while a prisoner in Cold Bath Fields a few months before. He was also a body-snatcher by occupation and a professional informer and *agent provocateur*. But, in their own way, they had deserved well of the medical profession by disinterring corpses for the Faculty of Medicine at Bart's. So when they were sentenced to death for burglary (the usual sentence at this time), the prosecutor and jury recommended the unsavoury pair to mercy.[24]

Finally, a few cases of collusion between criminals and people in the street, a fairly frequent occurrence where pickpickets were concerned. In December 1830, when Thomas Hall's shop was robbed of a tea-caddy (1s.), Hall's daughter Jane reported that when she grabbed the prisoner, a young labourer, 'three or four blackguard young men came up' and released him. On another occasion, when Edward Green,

23 *Proceedings*, 1830, nos. 557–8, 559–65; 1850, no. 1094.

24 *Proceedings*, 1810, no. 353; 1820, no. 411; 1830, no. 448; 1840, nos. 700, 1046.

a tea-pot manufacturer of Worship Street, was assaulted and robbed
of three silver dollars and 3s. on the King's Highway, 'several persons'
came forward (so the victim reported) and helped Samuel Cockbin,
his assailant, to knock him down. When Jonas Myers, a pencutter,
stole a watch and key from Golden Harridge, who was apprenticed
to a law stationer in Carey Street, the victim was 'ill-used by the
Mob'—twenty came up—who broke his jaw on the way to the watch
house. A third case involved Andrew Burn, a gas fitter, who stole a
handkerchief from Edward Springett in St John Street, opposite the
Cross Keys in the Borough Road. When the victim chased his
aggressor, 'the cab-man [so the victim reported] closed on him and
told him to run on—they stood between him and me'. On the other
hand—does this denote a change in popular attitudes towards criminal
and victim?—when Joseph Flemming, a labourer, stole a printed
book (4s.) from outside a bookshop in Museum Street, the prisoner
was chased and ran away 'from a Mob of people'.[25]

And now to return to the questions regarding female criminality,
briefly posed in a number of the passages above. We then saw (and
the point is underlined in Table 3.5 below) that there was a considerable variation in the proportion of women prisoners tried in the
different counties and courts. According to our samples, in the Sussex
quarter sessions 11.1 per cent of the prisoners were women, compared
with 11 per cent at the Gloucester quarter sessions and 9 at assizes,
and 22.3 per cent at the Old Bailey in London. We also saw before
that the partial evidence of the Agenda Books for the Sussex Assizes,
based on a more limited sample, suggests a mere 5 per cent, while at
the opposite extreme the returns of the Metropolitan Police Commissioners for 1832, 1840, and 1850 record that, in these years, the
proportion of women among prisoners brought before the London
magistrates' court rose to a figure varying between 33 and 35.7 per
cent, while falling back to 25 per cent in the case of the minority
committed for trial at quarter sessions or assizes. (These last two sets
of figures, owing to their incompleteness for the period as a whole, are
omitted from the Table.) What do these disparities suggest? In the
first place, they suggest that the proportion of women tried in the
'lower' courts (in this case, including courts of quarter sessions with
those of summary jurisdiction) is higher than the proportion tried in
assizes: this is clearly evident in the examples cited for Sussex and

25 *Proceedings,* 1810, no. 655; 1820, no. 411; 1830, no. 448; 1840, nos. 700,
1046.

London, though less so in the case of Gloucester. Why this should be is presumably that there was a tendency in many counties for the more serious, and more violent, crimes to be referred to assizes and that such crimes generally 'attracted' a smaller proportion of women. A further conclusion, however, which in some respects may appear to offset the first, is that, in London, female crime was more varied and more daring than elsewhere (this is already suggested by examples quoted earlier in the chapter) and that, therefore, the proportion of women tried there (though not necessarily convicted) tended to be higher than in the rural counties. This point is further underlined by the high proportion of female crime committed in the more 'urban' parts of the two rural counties: our Table shows that this 'urban' crime accounts for 77.4 per cent of cases tried in the Sussex sessions, 75 per cent of cases tried in Gloucester quarter sessions, and 65 per cent (perhaps a significant difference) at Gloucester assizes; it is, of course, a largely irrelevant factor in the case of London. Our Table also shows that there was a greater tendency for women prisoners to take action on their own account—that is, unaccompanied by other men or women—in the urban centres of the rural counties and that the proportion of 'unaccompanied' women varied between 75 and 77.4 per cent in the rural counties and rose to 92.5 per cent in the case of London. This may perhaps be another indication of the higher degree of independence and daring of female criminals in the urban—and, particularly, in the Metropolitan—context.

Another factor of some importance in this discussion is the nature of female crime. Does our investigation suggest a tendency for women to commit peculiarly 'feminine' crimes or to engage in some forms of criminal activity common to both sexes to a relatively lesser or greater extent than men? To take the second part of the question first. As we saw in the previous chapter, in both rural counties and London, larceny dominated all other types of crime that were brought to court: it accounted for 76.3 per cent of crimes tried at quarter sessions in Sussex; in Gloucester it rose to a little over 80 per cent at quarter sessions while falling (though still playing a dominant role) to under 50 per cent at assizes; and in London, it maintained a level of 75 to 83 per cent of all crimes between 1810 and 1850. In the case of women (as our Table shows), the proportion of commitments for larceny in the two rural counties was even higher: with an average of 81.2 per cent at quarter sessions in Sussex, 83 per cent (compared with 80) at Gloucester sessions and 65 per cent (compared with under 50) at

Gloucester assizes. Only in the case of London assizes were the proportions marginally reversed, with larceny forming an average of 72.3 per cent of all female crime, compared with one of around 75 per cent of all crimes for both sexes combined. A partial explanation may be that, in the rural counties, the range of crimes committed by women was more limited than that committed by men, whereas in London women played a more conspicuous part than elsewhere in such violent crimes as burglary, assaults, manslaughter, and robbery and engaged in a wider range of criminal activities (common to both sexes), including forgery or the passing of false coins (occasionally labelled 'misdemeanours'), fraud, bigamy, perjury, conspiracy, 'receiving', and embezzlement. One further crime remains for particular mention, as it was as peculiar to women as rape may be said to have been to men. This is 'infanticide', which included not only the wilful murder but the concealment of the birth or death of an infant child. Yet, with one exception, such cases as were brought to these courts, at least, were extremely rare, accounting in our sample for 2.1 per cent of cases tried at quarter sessions in Sussex, 0.6 per cent of those tried at quarter sessions at Gloucester, and 0.4 per cent of those tried at London assizes. The exception (as the Table shows) was the court of assize at Gloucester, where the figure rose to 8.4 per cent. Yet even here such cases generally ended, as they did elsewhere, in an acquittal or discharge.

The last point is of some significance in respect to female crime and criminality and prompts the wider question: were the courts inclined to be more lenient to women than to men? Some undoubtedly were. It is most striking in the case of Gloucestershire whose courts, in our sample, acquitted or discharged 42.7 per cent of women prisoners tried at quarter sessions and 45 per cent tried at assizes, whereas only 24.8 per cent of all prisoners brought to trial at this time were acquitted or discharged by the two courts combined. In Sussex and London these disparities were not so great: whereas the quarter sessions in Sussex and the London assizes both acquitted or discharged 23 to 24 per cent of all prisoners brought to court, the proportion of acquittals and discharges of women amounted to no more than 24 per cent in the first case and 25 per cent in the second.

Moreover, court records in Gloucester (more complete than those in Sussex) show that women were virtually never sentenced to be whipped (only 1 in 50 of all females committed); they were rarely placed in solitary confinement (3.5 per cent of women prisoners compared with 6.4 per cent of men); they had less than their fair share of previous convictions (6.6 per cent of women compared with 10.2 per cent of men); and they tended to be sentenced to shorter terms in gaol—to one to four months (or even six) but almost never (as more frequently with men) to five months or seven or eight. Yet, in Gloucestershire at least, women prisoners were as liable to be fined or sentenced to hard labour—and in almost identical proportions—as the men.[26]

In the case of transportation, it was the Old Bailey that stood out among these courts for the severity of the sentences it meted out to women. This was particularly so between 1820 and 1840 when the

Table 3.5 Female crime and criminality in the three counties*

	Sussex QS	Gloucestershire		Middlesex Assizes
		(a) QS	(b) Assizes	
	%	%	%	%
Women prisoners as % of all indicted prisoners	11.1	11.0	9.0	22.3
% Women charged with offences in 'urban' areas†	74.0	70.0	65.0	100.0
Crimes:				
committed by women acting alone	77.4	75.0	76.0	92.5
Larceny as % of female crime	81.2	83.0	65.0	72.3
Infanticide as % of female crime	2.1	0.6	0.4	0.4
Verdicts:				
Acquittals etc.	24.0	42.7	45.0	25.0
Transportation	1.9	1.8	5.4	23.4

* Based on the QS Order Bks., 1805–50, in Sussex; Prison Registers, 1815–50, in Glos; and OB *Proceedings*, 1810–50, in Middlesex/London.

† 'Urban' offences here refer to offences committed in the 25–30 most populated parishes in Sussex and Glos. (as listed in Appendices A and B below). The distinction is not applied to London (here portrayed, though not with strict accuracy, as being 100 per cent urban).

[26] Glos. Pris. Regs. 1815–50; Coll. W&M CC.

proportion of women sentenced rose from 15.7 per cent in 1810 to 27 per cent in 1830 and 25 per cent in 1840, while falling back (not unexpectedly) to 12 per cent in 1850 and with an average for the five sample years of 23.4 per cent. This compares, somewhat oddly, with the 1.4 per cent of women sentenced to be transported over this period at quarter sessions in Sussex and the 1.8 and 5.4 per cent recorded respectively by the courts of quarter sessions and assizes in Gloucester.[27]

Yet it is evident that such disparities do more than reflect the greater severity of sentences passed on women in the London assizes; they also reflect, to some degree at least, that greater variety, sophistication, and violence of female crime in the Metropolis that we mentioned above.

[27] Sussex QS Order Bks., 1805–50; Glos. Pris. Regs. 1815–50; OB *Proceedings*, 1810–50; Coll. W&M CC.

4

VICTIMS

1. SUSSEX

IN Sussex, a rural county but one with a considerable urban development along its coast, the major victims of crime could be counted among landowners (lords and gentry), shopkeepers, and farmers, and also among women and labourers, particularly those employed on farms. Indeed, if we turn to Table 4.1 we observe that labourers account for as many as one in eight of all the victims; and we shall also see from other evidence that, given the order of priorities displayed by larcenists, there were occasions when they offered as favourable a target as any.

Table 4.1. Victims of crime in Sussex 1805–1850 (as a percentage of all crimes at Quarter Sessions)*

Social Category	1805	1810	1815	1820	1825	1830	1835	1840	1850	Mean 1805–50
Lords, gentry	15.0	3.0	3.8	2.4	2.2	2.6	3.8	3.8	1.4	3.0
Shopkeepers, merchants	20.9	30.4	19.0	23.2	16.5	28.7	25.7	30.7	37.0	27.6
Farmers	20.9	20.3	15.2	21.6	18.9	21.6	18.3	22.2	16.7	18.9
Clergy	–	–	1.9	–	–	0.5	0.4	0.8	0.7	0.4
Women	9.0	9.0	4.8	4.8	9.0	8.6	9.0	7.0	9.8	9.1
Labourers	4.5	4.5	3.8	14.4	15.4	15.3	14.1	13.6	10.4	12.9
Craftsmen	3.0	–	1.9	3.5	5.9	3.1	2.1	0.4	0.4	2.0
Police	3.0	3.0	–	4.0	4.8	4.3	6.3	1.9	2.4	3.5
Miscell.	11.7	23.8	23.2	8.5	12.7	6.7	11.3	14.6	15.2	
Occupations unknown	12.0	6.0	26.4	17.6	14.6	8.6	9.0	5.0	6.0	10.3
	100.0	100.0	100.0	100.0	100.0	100.0	100.0	100.0	100.0	

* Sussex RO, Order Bks. 1805–50; QS Recognizances 1805–35 (incomplete). [Author's calculations.] No direct comparison can be made with assizes, as the Agenda Books give no details of victims and no occupation of prisoners before 1830.

To move from the bare statistics to the sort of losses suffered by different groups of victims we must turn to the Order Books of the Quarter Sessions. To begin with the labourers, who, as we saw, more often provided victims of larceny than we might have expected. The things actually stolen from victims, which we discussed in an earlier chapter, may perhaps provide a clue. We then saw that in Sussex (see p. 11 above) food, clothing, money and valuables, household goods, building materials, tools, and farm animals were the items that figure most frequently and most prominently on the larcenist's list of 'wants'. Among these, working clothes, tools, and fowls would be easily accessible to thieves in the homes and cottages of labourers and craftsmen. A few cases may illustrate the point. When, in September 1835, James Thompson (*alias* Hemmends) a labourer of Ticehurst, broke into the dwelling of James and William Bones, both labourers of Ticehurst, he helped himself to the following goods: two round-frocks worth 12s. (an indispensable item of the labourer's working attire), a waistcoat (6d.), a neckerchief (3d.), and a gold sovereign. The same defendant robbed another labourer's cottage three months later. This time the victim was John Balcombe, whose modest posses-sions were typical of what a labourer might expose to loss at this time at the hands of thieves or burglars. His losses included a watch (30s.), a knife (3d.) a tobacco box (2d.), and some silver and copper coins amounting to 2s. 10½d. The prisoner pleaded guilty on both counts and, having for the first offence been confined in 'solitary' for 14 days at the Lewes House of Correction, was now transported to Australia for life.

In September of the same year, Edmund Gladwin, another labourer, who lived close to the Kentish border, was robbed of a part of his bed linen and clothing when Julia Maria Cramp, described as a 'singlewoman', broke into his cottage at Bodiam and stole three gowns (20s.), two shawls (6s.), two shifts (2s.), a nightgown (3d.), an apron (1s.), two yards of cotton (4d.), a bed-quilt (2s.) and a gown cap (1d.); while, on the other side of the county, Peter Penfold, servant to Peter Sayers, a yeoman farmer, was robbed of a fowl, worth 1s., by Thomas Newnham, a labourer of Ardingley.[1]

Among lower middle-class victims was Alexander Rose, a victualler of Mayfield, who, in November 1824, had a pinafore (6d.), a pair of stockings (6d.), and two handkerchiefs (6d.) stolen from his house by Thomas Fuller, a labourer of the town. James Tupp, of Brighton, appears also to have been a tradesman; in January 1825 his house was robbed of three petticoats (4s.), three caps (9d.), two aprons (1s.),

---

[1] Sussex QS Order Bks., 1835; Recognizances, 1835.

and a handkerchief (8d.). In May 1840 George Adams, servant to John Waters, of Lewes, who may have been a professional man, stole from his master a watch key (2d.), two razors (2s.), a razor case (3d.), a musical snuff box (10s.), a locket (1d.), a book (2s.), two shirt-fronts (2s.), a pair of shoes (4s.), a tobacco box (1s.), and a pair of pincers (2s.), and, to complete his considerable haul, half a dozen other objects that may have belonged to his master's wife or daughter.[2]

Three labourers of Winchelsea got away with a richer prize when, in May 1835, they broke into the vessel *Unity*, lying in the Port of Rye under the command of James Hurssell, master mariner. They took three coats (£6), two jackets (£2), four pairs of trousers (£2), four waistcoats (30s.), two sheets (12s.), a pair of shoes (5s.), a pair of sea boots (£1), a table cloth (5s.), two towels (1s.), five pairs of stockings (5s.), six knives and forks (6s.), a pint of brandy (3s.), 10 oz. tea (4s.), 6 lb. sugar (3s.), and 6 lb. cheese.[3]

Finally, there were two rural crimes involving two farmers and a noble lord, a small-town crime involving a yeoman, and an 'industrial'-type crime which concerned the larceny of timber from a railway company. To take them in order of occurrence. In September 1815 three labourers of Westfield stole three pigeons, worth 20s., from the estate of Henry Lord Viscount Gage, a considerable landlord in those parts. In January 1829 two labourers of Bexhill stole twelve ducks (24s.), and two drakes (4s.) from Charles Brooke, a yeoman of the town. On 12 December 1839 two labourers and a woman stole a horse and a mare, valued respectively at £25 and £8, from John Cutler, a farmer of Petworth, West Sussex. And, in November 1840, James Collins, a labourer of Balcombe, stole an oak board (3s.) from the sleepers recently laid there by the London and Brighton Railway Company, the first railway to be constructed in Sussex.[4]

2. GLOUCESTERSHIRE

In the county of Gloucester, too, the principal groups of victims were gentry, shopkeepers and merchants, farmers, women, and labourers; but there were also new groups of householders and manufacturers of which we must take note. The Table of victims will give us a full

[2] Order Books 1825, 1840; Recognizances, 1825.
[3] Ibid., 1835.
[4] Ibid., 1815, 1830; Order Books, 1840.

picture of all victims that are worthy of being placed in distinctive categories. Table 4.2 gives us a full summary of these groups with their respective proportions.

Table 4.2. Victims of crime in Gloucestershire as a percentage of all crime 1815–50. QS and assizes combined*

Social Category	1815	1820	1825	1831	1835	1840	1845	1850	Mean 1815–50
Gents, lords	13.4	7.8	6.5	5.1	4.3	3.5	2.8	1.4	5.6
Shopkeepers	8.7	25.0	24.4	28.3	15.3	15.4	36.5	32.8	23.3
Merchants, manufs.	13.0	8.2	11.5	6.1	7.3	6.1	3.7	3.7	7.5
Farmers	19.6	15.2	19.9	16.3	17.2	16.7	26.1	21.9	19.4
House-holders	13.0	16.4	13.0	13.3	17.7	13.1	11.2	12.8	13.8
Labourers	8.7	10.2	9.5	9.7	2.3	1.1	3.7	1.6	5.9
Craftsmen	4.4	0.8	2.3	3.2	1.4	0.5	1.6	3.0	2.2
Police	–	–	0.4	0.5	–	0.2	0.2	1.8	0.4
Women (not already incl.)	6.5	3.9	3.1	5.1	7.8	11.2	5.1	9.1	6.5
Occupations unknown	10.9	10.9	7.0	8.0	23.8	11.0	6.3	8.2	10.8
Miscellaneous	1.8	1.6	2.4	4.4	2.9	21.2	2.8	3.7	–
	100	100	100	100	100	100	100	100	

* Glos. Pris. Regs. 1815–50 (author's calculations).

We find the same predominance of shopkeepers and farmers as before, but fewer women and labourers and the addition of two new groups of householders (13.8 per cent) and manufacturers and merchants (7.5 per cent). The householders (whom we shall also find, though in lesser numbers, in London) are those occupying dwelling houses other than farmers, shopkeepers, or labourers or craftsmen: they can be found here in significant numbers in Bristol, Cheltenham, Gloucester, and other centres of urban expansion. The manufacturers, of course, are the clothiers and millowners of Kingswood, Bisley, Painswick, Stroud, and Wotton-under-Edge, some of whose workers we saw engaging in 'industrial' crimes in two earlier chapters. The fall in the proportion of women is not due to any reduction in the number of women victims but only of those who are included in other groups. The proportion of women among all 2,500 victims listed in our sample from the sessions and assizes combined is a little under

10 per cent; but the proportion of women victims of certain types of crime, such as the assaults and rapes and larcenies counted as 'crimes against persons', is very much greater; they account for 49 such cases out of 112, or 43.8 per cent of the figures given.[5]

Among violent assaults on women the most traumatic, and most humiliating for the victim, was rape. Rape was a fairly common crime in the towns and villages of Gloucester at this time; yet the courts appear to have found some difficulty in deciding how to punish it. When, in April 1831, Eliza Waite, of Newnham, was raped by Samuel Nelmes, a moulder in an iron manufactory, the offender was given eighteen months in the penitentiary. But the Kingswood labourer who, nine months later, assaulted Harriet Brumble at Bitton, 'with intent to rape', received two years in the penitentiary at Cheltenham. This, too, was the sentence passed on Thomas Latham, a tailor, who raped Mary Ann Tuffly of Cheltenham. Fifteen years later, when William Gillespie, a smith and boilermaker, who had recently moved from his home in Devon to Stroud, assaulted and raped Susannah Crutchley, although described in his prison report as being given to drink and of a 'not very good character', he was given a term of no more than two months in the House of Correction. But, in August of that year (1845), an attempt by Thomas Donavan, an Irish gardener, to rape Sarah Leo at Cheltenham brought him a penalty of fifteen months in jail and a 1s. fine. However, neither the two months jail nor the fifteen months gives us any clear indication of which way the judicial wind was blowing; for, in May of that year, when John McGrath, a 37-year-old labourer who 'always went to Church', assaulted and raped Mary Ann Quinlan at Bristol, he was—inexplicably, it seems, as he had apparently no previous record of crime—sentenced to be transported for life.[6] We shall return to this strange phenomenon when we discuss the whole question of punishment in a later chapter.

We have seen that both clothing and tools were high on the list of priorities in the case of goods stolen in Sussex and Gloucester (see pp. 11 and 18 above). Clothing, including the traditional round-frock, was frequently stolen from labourers. Here are half a dozen examples from the sessions and assizes of 1820 to underline the point. When William Pearce, a sawyer and one-time soldier of the Royal Staff Corps, broke into the lodgings of George Knight, a labourer of

[5] Glos. Pris. Regs, 1815–50; Coll. W&M CC.
[6] Ibid., 1831, 1845.

Cheltenham, he stole a hat, a jacket, a pair of trousers, and a waistcoat; and when Ann Jones, 34, of Bristol, broke into Samuel Curry's house in the parish of St Philip and Jacob, she stole a yellow India silk handkerchief, worth 4s., and a muslin spencer (1s.).[7] Stephen Shore, 46, a former sailor and a Canadian from Quebec, stole a calico shirt from John Dennis, a labourer of Newport, on 22 July 1820, and spent a month in the penitentiary. Thomas Raffe, 23, of Chalford, took a silver watch from the house of Fred Nurse, a labourer from the parish of Saul; and Charles Godwin Smith, described as a 'navigator' (hence the modern term 'navvy') and formerly of the Division of Marines at Portsmouth, was sentenced at the Trinity Sessions to spend two months in the penitentiary for stealing four sheep skins from Peter Baradell, a labourer, at the parish of Withington.[8]

If clothing was often stolen from labourers, tools were more commonly stolen by one craftsman from another. We may take the case of Caleb Phelps, a shoemaker of Bisley, to illustrate the point. In July 1831 Phelps stole a pair of upper leathers, a pair of pincers, and 'a shoemaker's tool called a shoulder', the property of John Wheeler, shoemaker of Stow-on-the-Wold.[9]

If the theft of tools was the peculiar hazard to which craftsmen were exposed, in the case of landowners it was poaching under arms, sometimes the work of men who made a profession of the sport, sometimes that of enthusiastic, or hungry, amateurs. Here are three examples of poaching by urban craftsmen and village labourers, who probably belong to the second type. On 30 November 1824, Richard Clarke, a weaver of Stroud, entered a certain Lawrence Wood under arms 'with intent to destroy the game'; he was picked up by the gamekeeper who took him to court. On 4 January 1831 Robert Arter, a shoemaker of Broadway, was found poaching with a loaded gun on the property of Charles Hanbury Tracey, a landowner of Toddington; he spent eighteen months in the 'Pen'. And, in September 1845, George Ridler, a labourer of Bream, killed a fallow deer—a far more serious offence under the Game Laws than the two before—on enclosed ground that was occupied by Charles Bathurst, a gentleman of Lydney. The defendant's previous record is not very clear. One entry on the prison register gives him a clear record: 'never was in trouble before'; but a second entry adds: 'previously convicted at Summer

[7] A camisole.
[8] Ibid., 1820.
[9] Ibid., Summer Assizes, Aug. 1831.

Assizes 1842 and found guilty of assaulting a constable; 6 months in the Penitentiary'. This time he was given twelve.[10]

And, finally, the case of a woman householder who was the victim of the most dreaded scourge of the countryside, arson. At Coaley, on the night of 31 March 1845, Elizabeth Osborne, a labourer, aged 34, described as 'a bad character ... quite ignorant and very poor', set fire to the dwelling house of Susannah Bick. As the victim was in the house at the time, this rated as a capital crime and the prisoner, who had been jailed before, was first sentenced to death before this was commuted to a ten-year term of transportation, which in turn was followed, four years later, by a Free Pardon, sent to the prisoner in Tasmania, on 10 July 1849.[11]

3. LONDON

The main difference between London and the rural counties in respect of the victims of crime is not unexpected: the virtual disappearance of farmers and the consequent rise in the proportion of shopkeepers. Moreover, whereas in Gloucester merchants and manufacturers—the latter in particular—became important enough to play an independent role, this is no longer the case with London. So, in Table 4.3, these groups merge once more with shopkeepers, and thus help to inflate their numbers. In addition, householders, so prominent in our Table for Gloucester, show a marked decline, though this is not so much due to a fall in numbers as in their frequent appearance in these records under other occupations. The City of London's influence on the volume of crime has had two further results: the increase among victims of the proportion of craftsmen and the emergence of a small new category of clerks.

Behind the sombre figures lay a rich variety of victims, far richer of course in London than in either Sussex or Gloucester, or for that matter in any other region of Britain. First, there was Queen Victoria herself, who, as mentioned in an earlier chapter, was briefly menaced by the swish of a cane wielded by a former officer of the Hussars as she rode in procession through St James's. There was also the Emperor of Russia, though in his case there was no suspicion of any personal danger—only the embezzlement of two certificates in a Sinking Fund

10 Ibid., 1825, 1831, 1845.
11 Ibid., Summer Assizes, Aug. 1845.

Table 4.3. Victims of crime in Middlesex, 1810–1850 (as a percentage of OB crimes)*

Social Category	1810	1820	1830	1840	1850	Mean 1810–50
Gentry	2.1	4.8	1.6	3.2	3.5	3.0
Shopkeepers (also merchants, manufacturers, farmers)	48.0	42.8	48.4	50.2	50.2	47.9
Householders	2.0	2.4	5.3	4.0	3.7	3.5
Clerks	2.0	–	1.6	1.6	0.8	1.2
Labourers	7.5	7.3	6.6	6.4	3.8	6.3
Craftsmen	6.5	3.0	4.5	3.4	2.1	3.9
Women	7.5	8.8	9.4	9.0	13.4	9.6
Occupations unknown	18.6	12.7	15.8	15.5	17.8	16.1
Miscellaneous	5.8	18.2	6.8	6.7	4.7	
	100	100	100	100	100	

* OB *Proceedings*, 1810–50 (author's calculations). Neither the QS records nor the MPCR after 1831 have been of use in this matter.

bearing his name and converted by a certain Edward Nairne 'to an unknown use'. An aristocratic house was robbed of a £10 note by one Pleasant Neil, who had access to the Marquess of Donegal's town residence at 67 Eaton Place through the favours he enjoyed with a housemaid, Frances Biddulph. In our sample there are at least two Knights among the victims—Sir Frederick Beilby Watson, who was robbed of ten forks, six medals worth £22, two candlesticks, a pen-rack, and two pistols (£20) by his hairdresser, Henry Johnston Manbridge; and Sir Robert Burdett, one of four gentlemen-distillers of Vauxhall, who lost a five-gallon cask of brandy (£6. 5s.). The victims also included bankers and other heads or directors of business firms. Among the banks was the Commercial Bank of London, on which a false order for £10 was drawn by John Avan Broom, a 17-year-old clerk; while a larger amount—a bill of exchange for £100—was drawn by a drunken Naval captain on Sir John William Lubbock Bart's, a City banking house. The London Dock Company was robbed of a fishing rod, worth £2. 4s., by one of its employees, and the New River Co. of £5. 14s. by one of its labourers. The St Katharine Dock Co. thought it had lost 44 lb. of lead (5s.), but it was found in a privy branded with the Company's mark; while the Chartered Gas, Light and Coke Co. lost 2½ lb. of brass (1s.), but failed to secure a prosecution as its charter was not produced in court.

To turn to inland transport. James Sharp, a carman employed by the Grand National Junction Canal Company to carry goods to various parts of the city, kept some of the money collected and was given a three-month prison sentence for embezzling its funds. Although only one railway employee appears to have been involved, three London Railway Companies were the victims of crime: the South East Railway Company through the issue of a forged receipt for £7. 10s. by Henry Kelly, a builder; the Eastern Counties Railway Company was robbed of a wooden box containing 37 lb. of tea and 5 lb. of coffee (£9) by William Huslan, a labourer; and one of the London South West Railway Company's employees stole a purse (5s.) and its contents (6s. 1½d.).[12]

In May 1830 the Governors of St Bartholomew's Hospital (who have already figured in an earlier chapter) were robbed of 20 pairs of sheets, worth £7, 49 pieces of sheeting (20s.), 9 blankets (£2. 14s.), 20 yards of towelling (15s.), and several other items; the culprit, later transported for seven years, was Lydia Western, a sister at the hospital for the past nine years and living at Barrett's Court, in nearby Wigmore Street. Other 'charitable' victims included the Trustees of the Poor of St Leonard's, Shoreditch and the Directors of the Poor of the combined parishes of St George Bloomsbury and St Giles-in-the-Fields: the first was robbed of a guernsey frock (4s.), and the second of a sheet and four shifts (28s.) by an inmate who absentmindedly (it appears) walked out of the workhouse with one of its gowns on her back.[13]

There were distinguished foreigners among the victims, or at least some that bore distinguished-sounding foreign names. Two of these were Amédée Frédéric Armand Davenes and his brother Auguste-Nicolas Davenes, partners in a provision-dealer's in Turnmill Street that specialized in the sale of pigeons; the brothers were robbed of 21 dead pigeons, worth 12s. 3d., by two of their carmen. There was also Louis Henri Godineau, of the Union Hall at 33 Salisbury Square, who was robbed of his £15 watch by a prostitute, well known to the

---

[12] *Proceedings*, 1810, no. 187; 1830, no. 1,024; 1840, nos. 312, 314, 322, 328, 330, 348, 390, 550, 570, 580, 798; 1850, nos. 688, 1140, 1300, 1312, 1406, 1420, 1452. There was also among these notable victims, the case of *The Times*, which, in 1810, prosecuted 19 defendants on a conspiracy charge. Judgement was respited (see *Proceedings*, 1810, nos. 472–3).

[13] Ibid., 1830, no. 733; 1850, nos. 1428, 1606.

police, who took him up to her room one night in a notorious 'house of ill-fame' at the Temple. Among other such victims were Count Henri d'Avigdor, whose house at Acton was burgled one night of various goods amounting in all to a value of £4. 6s.; and Elizabeth, Margravine of Brandenburg-Anspach-Baireuth, who was robbed of two chimney pieces (£30), a pestle and mortar (7s.), and twelve books (6s.), removed from her Pavilion at Hammersmith by three men who lived on a barge. An unusual-sounding victim was 'Sheik Betchoo', who in July 1850 was robbed in a city brothel of two whistles (8s.), two handkerchiefs (3s.), and 1s. in cash. And, for good measure, among the overseas visitors to London there was Colonel Robert Anstruther of the Canadian Army, whose residence in Monmouth Road, Bayswater, was burgled of a snuff box and other objects, worth £16, by a plumber and a bricklayer who had been drinking in a neighbouring beer-house.[14]

Among victims of the 'middling' sort, we have already amply attested the dominating presence of shopkeepers; publicans, too, on a smaller scale were in evidence. The London publican had two occupational hazards, of which one was a rather heavier liability than the other. The lesser evil was the frequent removal of beer-mugs, then commonly referred to as pint beer-pots; and the larger was the passing of 'dud' coins or banknotes. Every Old Bailey session at this time witnessed at least ten or a dozen such cases; half-a-dozen of them often followed each other in rapid succession. Such was the case of Susannah Bennet, widow and licensee of the *George Tavern* at Snow Hill, who was passed a bad half-crown in 1840 but was astute enough to have the two defendants put in jail for twelve months; and of landlord Russell Poole, of the *Rose and Crown* in Bartholomew Close, in the Inner City, who was also passed a false half-crown and also brought his two assailants to justice. More serious was the loss of Isaiah Ralph, the publican of the *George the Fourth* of Edward Street, in Regent's Park, whose house was burgled in early 1850 for the loss of three quarts of brandy and 100 cigars, valued together at £3 in cash. The prisoner, an 18-year-old labourer living at Albany Place, was evidently something of a professional: he had already been sentenced to three months' prison at the Winter Assizes in December 1848 and would, a short while later, be convicted at the Old Bailey for the burglary of William Clark's public house, *The Jew's Harp*, also in

---

[14] *Proceedings*, 1820, no. 1024; 1830, nos. 330, 379; 1840, nos. 1572, 1756; 1850, no. 2098.

Regent's Park. On the two counts the young specialist in pub-breaking was transported to Australia for fifteen years.[15]

Many victims, as we have seen, were poor, either as wage-earning labourers or as part-time workers living on a depressed wage or allowance among the city poor. Some tried to hide it by investing in relatively expensive clothes. For example, when Richard Markson's lodging-house in Liquor-Pond Street, St Andrew's Holborn, was burgled in January 1830, Richard Yates, a labourer, was the principal victim. Yet his wardrobe, part of which was stolen, betrayed a man of relatively expensive tastes; it included a pair of trousers, worth 14s., a waistcoat (9s.), and two shirts (18s.), in addition to 17s. 6d. in cash. But this is probably an exceptional case; and it was certainly not true of the hats stolen by a gang of pickpockets in a Chelsea street in January 1820. A Chelsea pensioner, who was one of their victims, reported that the thieves were all wearing others' hats; and he added (ruefully, no doubt): 'The hats all appeared to belong to poor people.' Joseph James Castle, a carver of Bethnal Green, who was robbed of his watch in November 1840, earned no more than 6d. an hour and slept in his employer's workshop in Fleet Street. Thomas Cox, of Union Gardens, Kingsland Road, drove a cart for his wife who took in laundry. In October 1820 five pelisses (£2) were taken from his house. When he caught up with the thief in the White Horse in Fursby Street, he asked him, 'How d'you come to rob a poor man like me?' He received no reply to the question; whereas when Thomas Stephen Weston, who let apartments in Alie Street, Whitechapel, was robbed of a watch and chain by 'a well-dressed lady' who had come to look for a room, he asked her 'how she could rob such poor people as us'; and 'she said she did not give that a thought'. But sometimes prisoner and victim were in the same boat: when Benjamin Gitkins, a stonemason, who worked on a job in Mecklenburgh Square, put down his tools (nine chisels and a hammer) to go to lunch and had them stolen, he asked the culprit, 'what could induce him to rob a poor man like me?'; and the thief replied simply, 'it was through poverty that he did it'. Similarly, when John Wheeler, a carpenter, working at 10 New Street, in the City, was robbed of two planes (5s.), an oil-stone (2s.), and a square (18d.), the offender, a brickmaker, told him 'he was in great distress'. When Robert Harman, a bargeman, stole a coat (10s.), a pair of pants (5s.), two waistcoats (3s.), and 2s. 6d.

---

15 Proceedings, 1840, nos. 1154, 1594, 1720.

in cash from a barge on the Thames at Millbank, it turned out that
the principal victim was James Andrews, 'a poor boy', who begged the
thief not to take away the two quarter loaves he was taking home to
his mother. And when John Coles and his wife, drapers though
described as 'very poor', were robbed of five caps (5s.), three yards of
ribbon (1s.), and four handkerchiefs (3s.) by a visiting nurse, the wife
was seized for the rent while the husband went to the watch house
to see the prisoner wearing one of their caps![16]

What do we know about the characters or attitudes of the victims?
The answer is very little, far less than we know about some of the
garrulous prisoners whose remarks we caught in an earlier chapter.
Yet here and there we catch a glimpse of what they said or thought
about their relations with the prisoners. John Hill, a South Shields
mariner, who lodged in a sailors' home in London, was a cautious
man who thought he could outwit intruders. So, before going to bed
the night he was robbed, he counted his money in numbered notes,
tied them in a bundle with a rubber band before folding them into his
pantaloon and putting them under his pillow. Yet, for all his pre-
cautions, four thieves—three young women and a man—got in and
took away—presumably from under his pillow—£18. 10s. in notes.
Some victims were more spirited than others; like Sarah Stimson, who,
when she arrived by train from Chelmsford and was robbed of 6s. at
Shoreditch Station while waiting for a bus, challenged her thief in no
uncertain terms: 'You good-for-nothing fellow, you are robbing me!'
Some victims reacted more violently, and less good-humouredly, to
the persons who robbed them. When Robert Pite, a haberdasher, had
thirteen yards of ribbon, worth 10s., stolen from his shop by a 14-year-
old girl, he is supposed to have said 'he would hang this girl if he
could' and to have boasted that 'he had already hanged a man'. He
denied the accusations; and it may be that, quite unwittingly, his
intemperate outburst (or at least its reporting) helped the court to take
a lenient view of the crime, as the prisoner, although found guilty,
was merely fined 1s. and discharged.

On the other side of the barrier dividing criminals from victims
were those victims—and there were many employers among them—
who were extremely reluctant to prosecute: it is evident enough that,
except in the case of a serious crime, few employers would be willing
to send a good workman to jail. Such a workman was William Kirby,

---

[16] Ibid., 1810, nos. 374, 390, 483; 1820, nos. 510, 1970; 1830, no. 1672.

a butcher, who took 3¾ lb. beef and ¾ lb. suet from his master's shop in Goodge Street, Tottenham Court Road. The master butcher's wife, who ran the business, held the prisoner in high regard and at first refused to prosecute; but when, persuaded by the police, she agreed to do so, she gave him an excellent character. So the prisoner was recommended to mercy by both victim and jury and escaped with a month in jail.[17]

[17] Ibid., 1820, no. 431; 1830, no. 864. 1840, no. 1978, 1850, no. 1166.

5

TYPES OF CRIME

As the reader may have observed, this author has shown little inclination to follow the traditional division of crimes—dear to the criminologist and lawyer, if not always to the historian—into crimes against property and crimes against persons. If this distinction ever served a useful purpose—as it may well have done when England's rulers were most concerned to protect their rights of property in land —it may be said to be less so since Parliament became reformed and since the study of crime has become a matter of more frequent interest to the social scientist and social historian. In this chapter I propose to offer an alternative form of classification which may have greater relevance to present needs. Accordingly, it will be argued that there is some sense in dividing crime into three main categories: (1) *acquisitive* crime; (2) 'social' or 'survival' crime; and (3) *protest* crime, or protest made in breach of the law. Our earlier chapters relating to crimes, criminals, and victims have already suggested that these types are reasonably, if not wholly, distinct. (Some violent crimes, such as murder and rape, will not easily fit into any such scheme.)

Of these three the *acquisitive* and the *survival* type of crime are clearly the most closely connected and the most difficult to tell apart. So let us take them first and leave protest, as a more easily identifiable phenomenon, to the last. If we look back on our preceding chapters— particularly on the one that most specifically deals with 'Crime'—it may be readily seen that some of the crimes committed were concerned with the acquisition of wealth or property at others' expense—as a kind of investment without the trouble or expense of previous accumulation of capital assets. Some historians, in my view, have made the mistake of seeing the activities of the criminal involved in such an enterprise as a way of getting his own back by making 'war on society' as a form of protest or revenge for the ills he has suffered in a hostile world or society that has turned its back on him or rejected his needs. The fallacy is that the 'predatory' or 'acquisitive' criminal, who is merely concerned to line his pockets at another's expense, far from turning his back on acquisitive society, is accepting its norms— the norms of acquisitive capitalism which, by the early nineteenth century in England, was coming into its own, in fact not only accepting its norms but coming to terms with them in the manner most readily available to a man without property or means—that is, by larceny, burglary, robbery, or other forms of violent, or non-violent, self-help.

In this period, as we have seen, most crimes, whether committed in London or either of the two rural counties, come under the heading of larceny (or theft), whether larceny be on a small or a large scale. But where does one draw the line between larceny (or burglary etc.) for acquisition and larceny for survival? Partly it is a matter of the scale on which the larceny is carried out: a bank robbery or the burglary of a large shop or a rich man's house is clearly of a different order altogether from the theft of food, a set of tools, or a suit of clothes from a labourer's or craftsman's cottage. Partly, too, it is a matter of the purpose that underlies it: the object of acquiring wealth or capital, or of finding tools or materials to pursue one's craft, or money or clothes to buy food for one's own or one's family's survival.

So far, so good. But, more exactly, where (to repeat our question) do we draw the line? Let us go back briefly once more to the test that we applied to larcenists and burglars in the two rural counties of Gloucester and Sussex: what, in fact, did they steal? This might help to solve this part of our problem as well. We saw then the high priorities placed on the following: in Sussex on food, clothing, and money and valuables (in that order), accounting between them for 60 per cent of all items stolen; in Gloucester, on money etc., clothing, and food, accounting in this case for 52 per cent of the whole; and, in both cases, there was an additional 24 per cent accounted for by the theft of household goods (furnishing, bed linen, and the like), building materials, and tools. With the exception of money (a question-begging item if ever there was one), these are all typical means for survival for the labourer, craftsman, petty tradesman, or small consumer. In addition, among the most favoured items stolen, there were also farm animals and the means to feed them, amounting in both counties, when combined, to a further 8 per cent of all goods taken. These, too, like money could offer possibilities to the enterprising criminal for future investment and expansion. But when we examine the pages of the Order Books in Sussex or the prison registers in Gloucester, whether relating to quarter sessions or assizes, we find that, in all but a small minority of cases, the value of the animals or of the money stolen amounts to comparatively little. A common price of a horse or mare was £25, perhaps £8 to £12 for a gelding; add a few sheep, and the animals stolen from a farm or estate hardly ever account for more than £50; perhaps twice as much for a successful burglary of a large shop or an upper middle-class home in Brighton or Cheltenham. Add highway robbery or the larceny 'from the person' of a watch or a purse: in these the victim at most incurs a loss of £20 or £30; and even the forgery of banknotes and embezzlement of an employer's funds by trusted clerks or shopmen rarely amount, by the 1850s at least, to much more. These figures, set against the far greater volume of goods stolen in smaller quantities from farms and village homes and shops are likely to add up to only a small proportion of the sum total of crime.

In London the situation was evidently different: there were far greater opportunities, given the initial inclination, for thieves to concert together in pursuit of successful hauls. Above all there were, as we have seen, other forms of crime rarely seen in the villages or country towns. Coining and embezzlement played an altogether more important role and attracted men and women who, on occasion, became professionals at the game. The pickpocket, too, whose activities we have discussed at some length, tended to become a professional and to belong to a class of young thief of superior skills and intelligence, rarely drawn (it would seem) from the down-and-outs or the poorest of the poor. Burglaries, too, tended to be on a bigger scale. Yet the point should not be pressed too far. Our examination of the Old Bailey records suggest that, in London too, the *acquisitive* style of crime we have been discussing was here in a minority as well. A great deal of the typical London crime—the 'inside jobs' of servants, shop-men, and lodgers, and even the initiative shown by prostitutes in helping themselves rather than depending on the charity of their clients—all this also belongs to the quest for survival of the common-or-garden thief.

How do we put this survival motive to the test? If we were concerned to discover *trends* in the rise and fall of crime in general, and for that matter in the patterns of different types of crime, we might be tempted to rely on such objective factors as the rise and fall in the price of wheat or, if such facts were available to us, in the rise and fall of wages or earnings. But such a method, applied to the mid-nineteenth century at least, becomes fraught with difficulties, with other highly relevant factors tending to be left out: such as the level of employment in face of new industrial techniques; short-term variations in prices and regional variations in earnings, prices, and diets; the growing challenge of the potato as an alternative to bread; and (a crucial question) the proportion of earnings that the wage-earner, craftsman, or small tradesman spent on food both in the trough of depression and in the relatively more prosperous years that followed the worst of 'the Hungry Forties'.[1] So I shall prefer to rely on a more *subjective* test, based on the court records and drawing on the prisoners' own experience of poverty as an inducement to crime. For this purpose the Sussex records, whether relating to quarter sessions or assizes, are of little help; and the Gloucester prison registers only begin to be of service with the new information in the form of comments added in 1845 and 1850. My three Gloucester examples, in fact, belong to the year 1845. The first relates to George Cowley, a clothworker of Cirencester, described as being 'very poor', who was given a month's prison with hard labour for stealing a woollen shirt; the second to Thomas White, of King's Stanley, a carpenter by trade —but 'has done very little of late'—who was also given a month with labour for stealing two keys; and the third to Ruth Bale, a servant of Ridgeway and 'three months out of work', who served six months in the penitentiary for stealing a silver watch and chain.[2] Yet this is hardly a representative sample; so it is once more to the Old Bailey *Proceedings* that we must turn, with their numerous case-histories, to give us a far more comprehensive picture of the background to crime than we can find elsewhere.

Our evidence suggests that, in each of our selected decennial years, many prisoners at the London Assizes pleaded poverty as the prime cause of their crime and prosecution. In January 1810, Mary Macdonald, aged 37, with two fatherless children, pleaded 'extreme poverty' as the motive that prompted her to steal a brass cock, worth 2d., from John Rice who lodged in the same house; the court showed little sympathy, however, and transported her for seven years. It was

---

[1] G. Rudé, 'Protest and Punishment in Nineteenth-Century Britain', *Albion*, V (1973), part. 10–17. Macnab, however, argues convincingly that, throughout this period, the nationwide level of crime responded closely to short-term fluctuations in economic factors such as the level of employment and upward and downward turns in the business cycle ('Aspects . . .', pp. 295–394). Douglas Hay draws similar conclusions for the half-century before by using price-indices in relation to crime ('War, Dearth and Theft in the Eighteenth Century: the Record of the Courts', *Past and Present*, no. 95, May 1982, pp. 117–60). Both authors insist that the concordance was far stronger in the case of 'bread-and-butter' offences like larceny than in those involving violence.

[2] Glos. Pris. Regs., 1845.

more sympathetic to Daniel Burne, who, in the same year, claimed that he had been without food for four days before he stole a hat and an apron from a publican's potboy in St Marylebone; he was fined 1s. and discharged. Again, when Lewis Goulden stole two iron bars, worth 6s., from his former employer, an ironmonger of Upper Thames Street, and pleaded distress in mitigation of his offence, his victim agreed and he, too, was discharged with a 1s. fine. When Michael Moran, a labourer, stole two boards (4s.) from a carpenter of Red Lion Street, Holborn, he asked the officer sent to arrest him: 'What wouldn't a man do that had no victuals?'; but Thomas Gardner, a pickpocket who stole a handkerchief from a solicitor in Newgate Street, received little sympathy with his plea of 'distress' and was transported to Australia—the usual punishment for such a crime— for seven years.[3]

In March 1820, Atkinson Buck, a bookbinder, who stole a 3s. coal-tub from Edward Minton of Islington, told the court he did it 'for want of employment', which had reduced him to 'the most abject state of poverty'. In April William King, a florist, stole 24 pairs of gloves, worth 30s., from John Frazer, a haberdasher of Sloane Street; he excused his conduct by the 'hard times' and 'very bad trade' that his business had suffered 'since the King [George III] died'; he, too, was fined 1s. and discharged. When Henry Jones stole 45 yards of cotton and two yards of baize from his master's warehouse in Oxford Street, he told a tailor with whom he left the goods that he had been in a debtors' prison and stole to bring in money. In June, when William Kenton, a bricklayer, stole 1s., a 6d., and two £1 notes from the *Green Dragon* in Cripplegate, he told the publican that he had a large family to feed and was out of work. When James Hunt stole a watch, chain, seal, and compass from the person of John Shurm, a glass-cutter of Doctor's Commons, he explained he was 'out of work' and 'in great distress'; and William Day, who stole a basket, a rope, and a whip from John and Samuel Whitbread, farmers at Edmonton, told his victim he 'was starving'.[4]

The year 1830 was the most 'distressful' year of all. When, at the end of December 1829, John Butler, a saddler, stole a chaise harness, worth £6, from Thomas Arber of Bentinck Street, Manchester Square, he told the pawnbroker with whom he pledged it at the cut-down price of 22s. that he was 'in distress' and so poor that he must pawn

3 OB *Proceedings*, 1810, nos. 192, 277, 317, 397, 443, 444.
4 *Proceedings*, 1820, nos. 303, 430, 582, 769, 779, 1054.

it. Mary Downs, who occupied a furnished room at 3s. a week, stole a sheet worth 4s. from Alexander Smith, her landlord, in Portpool Lane; she too pleaded 'distress'. Also in December 1829, William Norman, a shoemaker, took 20 rolls of bread from the window of a Shoreditch baker's; he had (he said) been three weeks without work and one or two days without food. Ann Smith, a 61-year-old widow, who stole a 3s. tub from a shop on Eyre Street Hill, told the court she was 'in great distress and could get no relief'. Thomas Jones, a carpenter, who stole 5 lb. of pork from a butcher's in Lincoln's Inn Fields, explained that he had had 'no work for some time and no victuals for 2 or 3 days'. William Jones, a labourer, who was charged with stealing a 4s. handkerchief on Ludgate Hill, was 'looking for a situation' at the time. Thomas Barnes, a carpenter, who, in February 1820, stole a coat and a memo book from a hotel-keeper in Adam Street, Adelphi, told the court in his defence that he had been 'out of work a great part of the winter' and had a wife and two children, 'but not a morsel of bread'. When Henry Brown, a cabinet-maker, stole a sausage machine (50s.) from an ironmonger in Wardour Street, he said he intended to replace it 'as soon as he got work'; Charles Grace, a painter, had also been 'looking for work' when he stole four brushes (8s.) from Leonard Dell, a shopkeeper in St Martin's Street. Jane Allun, who stole two sheets (3s.), a blanket (3s.), a quilt (1s. 6d.), and a flat-iron (1s.) from the house where she lodged, pleaded 'distress and want'; she had four children and a husband out of work. She was recommended to mercy and confined for seven days. When George Wilkins stole a handkerchief from Margaret Goff in a lodging house, he pleaded that 'starvation and hunger drove [him] to it'. And when Christopher O'Hara, of North Street, St Matthew Bethnal Green, assaulted John Trapp, a printer, it turned out that the victim was his landlord with whom he was in arrears over the payment of rent.

And so we can continue with the long saga of distress through late February to December 1830. In February again, Elizabeth Bumstead, a widow with six children, who had taken pewter pots from public houses in St Marylebone and Camden Town, asked the court, 'how could she provide for them?'; and Thomas Goodall, a butcher, stole four loaves from a chandler's shop because 'he was very hungry and had no food for two or three days'. In March, a millwright, who had stolen timber, said he was in 'a state of starvation' with a wife and two small children to support; and, in April, a labourer, who had stolen a beehive and 10 lb. of honey, said he was 'out of work with nothing to eat'; a painter stole three loaves from a baker in Wild Street—he was 'out of work and [had] a large family in distress'; and Mary King, a widow, who stole two gowns, a frock, and a pinafore from a house in Somerstown, said she was 'tempted . . . being without a shilling'. William Kerry robbed a fellow-lodger and fellow-labourer of 4d., while he slept, in order to buy bread; and, in June, John Christian, who robbed his landlords of two sheets, a pillowcase, and a window curtain, said 'they have known I have wanted bread and never offered me a loaf'.[5]

There were a few more cases of this kind in the late months of 1839 and in early 1840, when the price of the quarter of wheat, having reached a seasonal peak of over 70s. in the summer and autumn of 1839, was still—at 66s. 4d.—relatively high.[6] In September 1839, when George Moore stole a suit of clothes from a fellow-tailor with whom he lodged, he claimed he was 'out of work'; and, in December, when Sarah Saunders took 1s. 6d. worth of beef from a butcher's stall in Brick Lane, Spitalfields, it was said in court that her husband was 'a hard-working man' but both were 'in distress'. And in the same month, Henry Turner, an unemployed sailor who stole a jacket from a ship in port said that he was 'in distress' as he had failed to be taken on as an apprentice, and he added (as others had done before him), 'I did it on purpose to be transported' (but, in fact, he was only jailed for six months).[7]

Several more such cases follow in 1850, when the price of wheat was low but the level of unemployment continued to be high. In March a cook stole a watch, 'being in great distress'; a labourer, who stole two pewter pots from a pub, said 'he was out of work since Christmas', that his wife and two children 'had nothing to eat', and that he would sell the pots 'to get a loaf of bread'; and Ann Davis, known to be 'very poor', stole a shawl and pawned it as she was 'in great want'. In April a labourer who stole a handkerchief from a stranger in Shoreditch said he was 'looking for work'; and an unemployed house-painter, who stole three planes and a saw, was 'tempted to [do so] to get a loaf for [his] children'. In May a bricklayer's labourer stole five iron bars 'to get [as he said] a drop of beer'; and a 13-year-old boy, who stole a pair of gaiters (7s.) from a gaiter-maker

5 Ibid., 1830, nos. 318, 384, 410, 434, 446, 516, 530, 532, 550, 556, 582, 636, 678, 742, 806, 820, 842, 866, 918, 920, 940, 1012, 1072, 1144, 1194, 1212, 1298, 1312, 1322, 1380, 1660, 1746, 1752, 1756, 1928, 1944, 2054.

6 Rudé, 'Protest and Punishment . . .', p. 11.

7 Proceedings, 1840, nos. 480, 492, 600, 626, 684.

in Leicester Square, sold them to a City broker for $2\frac{1}{2}d$. (he refused to pay him $3d$.!), as 'his father wanted bread'.[8] This is not the end of the list: there were at least a dozen more in my sample through the months of June–October that year; but what has already been said should amply suffice to establish that such crimes, illustrated in such large numbers in the *Proceedings*, properly belong to a category that may for convenience, and with reasonable exactness, be defined as 'survival'.

Of quite a different order, of course, is the type of crime that historians of the late paternalist society of eighteenth-century England have termed 'social'.[9] The criminal activities so defined, often involving an appeal to tradition or 'common rights', have included deer-hunting in Windsor Great Park, smuggling, poaching, sending anonymous letters, and rescuing the hanged bodies of malefactors from the depredations of barber-surgeons and anatomists at Tyburn—all crimes which, though most definitely proscribed at law, at one time enjoyed a community, or 'social', sanction. It is a useful and relevant distinction to make, particularly in the mainly rural and still paternalist society to which these authors have applied it. But it is not quite so relevant in the context of the present book, not only because 'Tyburn's Fatal Tree' was no longer standing at this time, but also because smuggling and poaching—like rural incendiarism and threatening letters—were losing their community appeal, and again because that relevance had never been so great in the case of London as in that of the rural counties where, as we have seen, poaching and smuggling still survived; though, after 1830 at least, not on the same scale, or with the same appeal to tradition, as fifty or a hundred years before.

There remains to consider protest or 'protest' crime with which 'social' crime has been sometimes confused. They are not the same thing. Both 'social' crime and protest in breach of the law are social acts in the sense that they are not largely prompted by an acquisitive urge; but protest is also a *collective* act (as, to confuse the issue, smuggling is, too), though it may not always be carried out in the company of others. Such acts are fairly easy to recognize in the case of trade-

---

[8] *Proceedings*, 1850, nos. 296, 444, 716, 894, 924, 940, 984, 1218, 1276, 1362, 1662, 2244, 2458, 2470, 2592, 2644.

[9] See, in particular, D. Hay, P. Linebaugh, E. P. Thompson *et al.*, *Albion's Fatal Tree: Crime and Society in Eighteenth-Century England* (London, 1975); see, also, C. Emsley, 'Crime and the Police', in *Policing and its Context 1750–1870* (London, 1983), pp. 115–31.

union militants, machine-breakers, food-rioters, demolishers of fences, turnpikes, and workhouses, administers or receivers of unlawful oaths, treasonable or seditious persons, armed rebels, and city rioters—all those, in fact, who generally protest within the context of a 'popular movement'. But there are others as well, not so easy to distinguish, whose activities belong to that shadowy realm between crime and protest where it is often not easy to tell them apart and also, as one must add, where protest and 'social' crime (in the Albion sense) often come together. I refer in particular to such types of marginal protest as rural incendiarism, poaching and smuggling, cattle-maiming, assaults on persons in authority, and the dispatch of anonymous letters. Here there are no easy blanket definitions to fall back on and each case has to be judged on its merits, and a distinction clearly made, for example, between one type of assault and another and between an act of arson to claim insurance and one that is an act of reprisal against a landlord, employer, or parson.[10]

But, in the context of this book, there will be no such problem of selection. We have already, in earlier chapters, touched on such marginal types of protest as arson, cattle-maiming, and the destruction of metal traps; but here we shall consider as our example an act of collective protest whose purpose was very clear—the breaking of threshing machines, accompanied by riots over wages and Poor Law allowances and rural incendiarism—that swept through our two rural counties in the great labourers' revolt in the autumn and early winter of 1830. The 'Swing' riots (as they have become called) started with the destruction of machines and demands for higher agricultural wages in East Kent in August, and spread into the Kentish and Sussex Weald in October, where they became compounded with wages riots, arson, and attacks on workhouses and Overseers of the Poor. They spread with remarkable speed, rarely lingering in any one county, after their initial impetus in Kent, for more than a few days. They moved west into West Sussex, Hampshire, Wiltshire, touched Dorset and Hereford, and stayed four late-November days in a score of villages in Gloucester. From Berkshire a new wave spread back east and north into Buckingham, Oxford, and Northampton; and another, starting on the Norfolk coast, spread south to Norwich, into Suffolk (where Church of England parsons became a major target over tithe), and into Essex (over wages) before moving back west and north into

[10] For a fuller discussion, see my Protest and Punishment (Oxford, 1978), pp. 3–7.

Cambridge, Leicester, and Lincoln, with a final northern convulsion (limited to threatening letters) in the region of Carlisle. In all, before the riots subsided in early December, sixteen counties had been more or less seriously affected, leading to the trial of nearly 2,000 prisoners by 90 courts sitting in 34 counties; of these 19 were executed, 694 imprisoned, and 481 transported to Australia.[11]

Here, of course, we are only directly concerned with our two rural counties, Sussex and Gloucester; London, not surprisingly in such a case, remained untouched. The main trials were those of 74 Sussex men at the Lewes Assizes in December 1830 and of 91 Gloucestershire men at the Michaelmas Quarter Sessions at Gloucester in January 1831. In Sussex 41 of the 74 prisoners were charged with having engaged in a variety of 'Swing' activities: in machine-breaking, in riots over wages, taxes, and tithe, in assaults and the extortion of money, in the forcible recruitment of labourers, in sending anonymous letters, and in dumping Poor Law officials over the parish border. Among them there were 28 labourers, a gardener, a hoopmaker, a school-master and nine craftsmen. Their average age was 30 years and 6 months. Gloucester's 91 prisoners were all charged with similar offences—but mainly with breaking agricultural machinery, and with riot and assault. There were 79 labourers among them and a dozen craftsmen; their average age was 27 years and a month. So they were younger than the Sussex men but still significantly older than the average of the prisoners brought to trial in Gloucester-shire over these 40 to 50 years (see p. 45 above). From the two counties 17 Sussex men and 27 Gloucester men were sent to Van Diemen's Land (the present Tasmania) for varying terms. But, what-ever the length of their sentence, it is doubtful if any of these 44 exiles ever returned to England and, while some may have migrated to the mainland for the Gold Rush of the 1850s, it is probable that they all remained in Australia for the rest of their lives.[12]

The victims of the riots were mainly farmers, landlords, and parsons. To be more precise, in Sussex, they numbered 25: among

11 E. J. Hobsbawm and G. Rudé, *Captain Swing* (London and New York, 1968), *passim*.

12 *Sussex. A Calendar of the Prisoners for Trial at the Gaol Delivery to be holden at Lewes on Saturday 18 Dec. 1830*. PRO ASSI. 35/270. Gloucester Prison Registers, 1815–71. Hobsbawm and Rudé, *Captain Swing*, pp. 265–80, 308–9. It was common for convicts transported for protest to be older than the common run of convicts, and also more married and less involved in previous and subsequent offences (Rudé, *Protest and Punishment*, pp. 242–7).

them twelve farmers, two gentlemen, one noble lord (the Earl of Sheffield), a parson, two Overseers of the Poor, and three labourers who were forcibly recruited to join the rioter's ranks. Among Gloucester's fifteen victims there were twelve farmers, a papermaker (who had his machinery broken), a police officer, and a parson. So there was a distinct antithesis (far more evident than in other forms of crime at this time) between the wage-earning labourers and craftsmen, threatened with reduced allowances and wages and the loss of work, and the community of landlords, farmers, and parsons who, whatever their differences over rents and tithes, had a common purpose in reducing labour costs by cutting allowances, standing down 'redundant' labour, or employing machines.[13]

---

[13] Admittedly, this places a slight over-emphasis on the antagonism between the labourers and the smaller farmers who, in some counties, had little interest in using machines and even co-operated with the labourers in breaking them or bringing pressure on landlords, tax-collectors, and parsons (*Captain Swing*, part. pp. 223–38). This was a familiar feature in East Anglia and in the Sussex Weald, but evidently not so in Gloucester, Hampshire, Berkshire, and Wiltshire. So, in general, the argument used in the last paragraph of the chapter is valid enough.

6

DETECTION AND POLICING

BEFORE Peel's reforms of the 1820s and 1830s there were two great obstacles, applying to both the metropolis and the provinces, standing in the way of bringing malefactors to justice. One was the system of private prosecutions, the other the lack of a metropolitan police force or any national organization for co-ordinating the police forces in the boroughs and counties.

The first problem was still a matter of some concern when the century began; for at that time there was no regular and assured means of compensation from which the prosecutor (who was generally the victim), nor his witnesses nor the police could be suitably compensated for the cost, time, and trouble involved in bringing a suspected prisoner to court. Moreover, the savagery of the law (before Peel's review of the penal code after 1827) was such that many a victim of larceny, in particular, would hesitate to play a part in inflicting a capital sentence for a comparatively minor property offence. Such men's objections were summed up in the report of the *Select Committee on the Police of the Metropolis in 1817* as follows:

The only impediments that are met with upon the general subject of legal prosecutions are of two kinds. First, the expenses of the prosecution. Secondly, the severity of the laws, which often deter men from pursuing the offender to conviction.[1]

It was in direct response to this report that, even before Peel's term of office, an Act of 1818 empowered the courts to award an allowance for loss of time and trouble and expense to all prosecutors and witnesses in all felony cases; but it excluded misdemeanours, which covered most assaults, perjury, riot, coining, and obtaining property under false pretences—all offences, as we have seen, that played an important role in both provincial-urban and metropolitan crime at this time. This last serious omission was largely rectified by Peel's Criminal Justice Act of 1826, which extended the system of recovering expenses to include most of these misdemeanours; it also made it possible for parish constables (the most important peace officers at parish level at this time) to recover the cost of detaining suspects in

[1] Cited by D. Philips, *Crime and Authority in Victorian England*, p. 113.

custody and bringing them to gaol and court without being dependent
for compensation on the good graces of the rich. This Act, as we saw
before (p. 26 above), also released a great spate of prosecutions by less
prosperous victims. Further, the final deterrent to prosecution—the
fear of the undue severity of the law—was also overcome by Peel's
and Russell's reforms of the penal code: by 1837 the death penalty
had been repealed for all offences against property (including
burglary).[2] Yet the system of private prosecution, with its lack of
effective guarantees of compensation, remained a certain deterrent to
prompt action by the poorer class of victims to bring their robbers and
assailants to justice.[3]

The other obstacle to effective detection and prosecution of crime
lay in the continuing archaic system of policing that had survived
from medieval and Tudor times. The parish constable was still the
linchpin of that system, both in the provinces and in London. In
London it was buttressed by a more sophisticated array of local
magistrates, marshals, and beadles supported at street level (and this,
of course, included our rural counties) by the watch and ward of the
parishes and precincts in which, nominally, all citizens played a part.
While the system became to some extent professionalized by the
levying of a regular watch rate and the payment (in larger parishes
and towns) of a small number of salaried officers, it still bore, and long
continued to bear, the stamp of its medieval, strictly amateur, and
parochial origins. Such a force had the undoubted advantage of drawing on local initiative and of being firmly rooted among its citizens.
The right of local defence (in which policing was an important
element) was a jealously guarded tradition, particularly in the City
of London where any suggestion of a *metropolitan* or national system
had been long and sternly resisted as an invasion of local privilege
by the executive power. Moreover, the old system worked reasonably
well in the case of purely local crime. But, of course, it was quite
unsuited to deal with a major conflagration (as in the Gordon Riots
of dreaded memory), for its essentially parochial nature impeded
magistrates in tracking down offenders across parish boundaries, let
alone across such major administrative frontiers as those separating
the City of London from Westminster or the old Bills of Mortality
from the near-rural hinterland beyond.

---

[2] Macnab, however, discounts the reluctance of victims to prosecute owing
to the harshness of the law ('Aspects of the History of Crime . . .' pp. 80–163).

[3] Philips, pp. 110–16.

At base level and most familiar to the public was the watchman, or 'Charlie' (he went back to Charles II's time), with his whistle and rattle that it was his duty to blow or to 'spring' when he needed assistance. It seems doubtful, however, if he commanded much respect among those he was supposed to apprehend. In May 1820, when three men were stealing lead off a roof in Stepney, one was heard to call to the watchman on duty: 'If you come at us, you old B–ger, I'll knock you down'. So he 'sprung his rattle' to summon help. Another watchman, who still depended on the old methods of alert (this was in April 1830, a month before recruiting began to the New Police), also 'sprung his rattle' when he called the police to arrest a labourer caught stealing a copper from a building in Little Queen Street, Mayfair. In September 1820, when a coachman, intent on robbing a 'poor woman' in a public house, whistled for help, a dozen hackney coachmen responded, and the watchman, in the face of such numbers, failed to intervene. Similarly, the watchman had no authority to chase a thief across a parish boundary (in the City, with its multiplicity of parishes, this naturally created problems!). In October 1820, for example, a victim of a pocket-picking operation in Whitechapel, having grabbed one of his two assailants, found the attending watchman unwilling to follow suit: 'I secured Smith [he testified later], but the watchman would not take her as it was not on his beat, so I let her go.'[4]

Yet, for all its inadequacies, the night watch afforded some protection and some degree of security in the parishes in which it appeared at reasonable strength, while in others the watch was entirely inadequate or did not exist at all. Thus, while St James's, Marylebone, and Hackney were conspicuous for their well-regulated watch, other large parishes—they included Kensington, Fulham, and Deptford—had no such protection at all and, on the very eve of Peel's reforms, it was reported of Spitalfields (a substantial borough with a population of 18,000 in 1830) that gangs of thieves 'stood at the corners of the streets, robbing, in the middle of the day, all persons who came within their reach . . .'[5] In these and other areas, it is true, some protection was afforded by such moveable forces, going back to the previous century, as the Bow Street Runners, the House Patrol, and the constables attached to the Police Offices established at Bow Street, Wapping, and elsewhere. In theory, the Bow Street House Patrol

4 OB *Proceedings*, 1820, nos. 681, 917, 1332; 1830, no. 886.
5 Sir Leon Radzinowicz, A *History of the English Criminal Law and its Administration* (4 vols., London, 1948–68), IV, 158.

protected the high roads within twenty miles of the Metropolis, while
its Dismounted Patrol protected its suburbs and its Foot Patrol the
city streets. But, in practice, the whole Night Foot Patrol amounted,
in the late 1820s, to no more than a hundred men, the day patrol
to a mere twenty-five, and the combined strength of Police Office
constables, Runners and Foot and House Patrols to only 300.[6]

Moreover, there was no systematic method of detecting crime in
London until the Whig reformers, following Peel, created the first
professional detective force in 1842. In the meantime, detection was
left to the plain-clothes police, directed from the Police Offices, who
called to their aid the resources of a familiar but thoroughly un-
professional institution. This was the pawnbroker's shop, later supplemented, or succeeded, by the marine-store shop, which dealt in
second-hand goods. The pawnshop performed a useful, dual, function.
On the one hand it provided the thief with a convenient means of
exchange for his ill-gotten gains of jewellery, curtains, and bed-linen
which, having made his escape, he pledged or traded for money. On
the other hand the pawnbroker's shop, precisely because it offered
such ready opportunities for thieves, was under close police surveillance, and the pawnbroker was expected to report all suspicious
transactions and to attend at court in order to bring committed
persons to justice. In fact, in the *Proceedings* for March 1830 we find
the case of a pawnbrokers' refusal to attend a police hearing incon-
venient to themselves—much to the indignation of the prosecutor
who charged that the pawnbrokers, by not attending at the proper
time, '[had] done everything they could to prevent this prosecution'.[7]

A few examples follow, from different times and in different parts
of London, to illustrate this role of the pawnshop in the detection of
crime. In December 1809, Elizabeth Stent, who worked for a milk
distributor, stole a coat, a handkerchief, and a shawl, worth about 10s.,
and on the same morning pawned each item with James McGuire, a
local pawnbroker who, convinced that the goods were stolen, reported
the matter to the police. In February 1810, Elizabeth Wilson, a
servant, stole a tablecloth (3s.) and a sheet (4s.), a flat iron (6d.), and
a tea-spoon (1s.) from her employer, John Butler Saunders, in Clerkenwell; the pawnbroker's certificates were found in her pocket and
helped to convict her. When, in December of that year, Susannah
Jenkins, a singlewoman, stole a coat worth £4 from the dwelling house

6 Radzinowicz, IV, 158–9; Macnab, p. 164.
7 *Proceedings*, 1830, no. 1214.

of William Adkins, a governor of the Middlesex House of Correction, she pawned it for a quarter of its price with Samuel Wright, pawnbroker of Mutton Hill. The same month, St Bartholomew's Hospital, in the City of London, became once more the victim of larceny when Eliza Parrot, a nurse, stole a sheet (3s.), having previously pledged two others but redeemed them. A pawnbroker of Snow Hill had handled both transactions and paid her one third of their value. In March Susannah Taylor stole two sheets (10s.), two blankets (22s.), and a bolster (12s.) from the room where she lodged in Featherstone Street, in the City. Although she dispersed her takings over three pawnshops, one in Old Street and two in Whitecross Street, she was caught and given a year in the House of Correction.

There were also several pawnbrokers involved from the Tothill Fields area when, in May 1810, Freeman Martin stole a gun (10s.), a silk pelisser (7s.), two sheets (5s.), and a shawl (2s.) from his lodgings in King's Row, Pimlico. John Warren appears to have been an old hand at the game, as, when he stole a coat worth 4s., the property of Medicus Ramsgate, a butcher, from a cart in Leadenhall Market in August that year, he was found with 20 pawnbrokers' duplicates in his pocket. Humphrey Pane, an errand boy, who stole jewellery worth 48s. from a working jeweller in Fetter Lane, was found with eight duplicates when arrested; while John Prickett, a silversmith, who stole £10 worth of silver from his master in Compton Street, Clerkenwell, was found with 23. Rebecca Goodyear, who lived with Mary Ann Thompson in Grosvenor Street, Westminster, as a kind of companion (she claimed that she shared her clothes), did even better: she had no fewer than 50 pawnbroker's duplicates in her possession when arrested for making off with a shirt (7s.), two pairs of stockings (4s.), and a teapot (2d.). But she put up a strong defence, saying that half the duplicates belonged to her and, being found guilty of no more heinous offence than stealing a tin box worth 2d., she escaped with a six-months' term in the House of Correction.[8]

By 1830, the day of the pawnshop as a combined means of exchange and semi-official detection was almost past; and, for a while in the 1830s and 1840s, the marine-store shop appears to have taken its place; but recorded examples from the Old Bailey *Proceedings* are admittedly few. In January 1840 William Davis, a labourer, who had taken a spring balance worth 10s. from Robert Johnston's shop in St

[8] Ibid., 1810, nos. 266, 384, 390, 434, 670.

John Street, City Road, said he intended to sell it at a marine-store shop but (mysteriously) lost it on the way. When William Lane and William Morgan, both coopers, took 90 lb. of lead (11s.) from Joseph Wilkinson's house in Fleur de Lys Court, in Watling Street, they took it to sell at the marine-store shop at the junction of Ratcliffe Highway and Chigwell Hill; and Ann Dawsey, who had taken seven iron bars worth 5s. from an iron merchant's in the Edgware Road, brought them to sell at a marine-shop nearby, claiming that they were 'surplus rails' she had found on a heap of rubbish.[9]

But the marine-store shops soon came under suspicion as being more inclined to be receivers of stolen goods than allies of the police in the detection of crime. So we find a number of these dealers, or their agents, being charged with such practices at the Old Bailey in 1840 and 1850. When William Monk stole 12 lb. of leaden pipe from his master, a plumber in the Mile End Road, he took it to John Beckett's marine shop for sale. Beckett was subsequently charged with 'receiving' and both men were sent to prison for fourteen days. In August 1840, Jane Powell, a marine-store shopkeeper of Playhouse Yard, was convicted of 'receiving' three pairs of shoes (5s.) and a pair of boots (3s. 4d.) which a young apprentice had stolen from William Tillinghurst's shoeshop in Brick Lane; but she was given a good character and confined for only fourteen days. In 1850, Thomas Evans and Richard Stewart, partners in a marine-store business on St Andrews Hill, were charged with 'receiving' eighteen sacks, worth 22s., the property of Thomas Reeve Denny, a corn merchant of Upper Ground Street, Blackfriars; yet, for lack of evidence, the case was dismissed. But George Steven Davis, a marine-store dealer of Compton Street, was less fortunate: found guilty of 'receiving' 75 metal castings, worth £6. 3s., stolen from Charles Butter, a prosperous brass-founder and engineer of Clerkenwell, he was given a twelve-months' term in jail.[10]

Outside London, the whole system of policing and detection remained at a far more primitive stage. The old parochial methods, based on the traditional watch and ward under the direction of the parish constable, still prevailed—except (as we shall see) where voluntary initiative had been harnessed to augment them. Our two rural counties were no exception; and, inevitably, it was the urban areas within them that suffered most from the existing inadequacies. Bristol, in spite of its great mercantile wealth, was, at its grass-roots, one of

---

[9] Ibid., 1840, nos. 702, 2100, 2568.
[10] Ibid., 1840, no. 1634; 1850, nos. 462, 1148, 1308.

the poorest and most disease-ridden cities in the Kingdom. In 1801, when a labourer could earn little more than 8s. or 9s. a week, the price of bread rose to 1s. 10d. for the quartern loaf, leading to serious riots in the city's markets; following the Spring Assizes, three convicted rioters were hanged at Bristol, six at Gloucester, and nine at Taunton. Thirty years later, in the wake of the notorious riots of 1831, the city's non-elected Common Council ventured to take a first step towards establishing an adequate force by setting on foot a body of a dozen day constables, to be paid a wage of 15s. a week at a total charge of £468. But even this modest sum aroused intense resentment among the ratepayers, and a parliamentary report on municipal corporations presented in 1835 related that 'at Bristol, a notoriously ineffective police cannot be improved, chiefly in consequence of the jealousy with which the Corporation is regarded by the inhabitants'.[11] Meanwhile, Brighton, by now the most substantial town in Sussex, was faring no better; and one of the city's more recent biographers reports contemptuously that its rising crime rate in the 1820s led to the establishment of 'a police force of a sort' in 1830.[12] In both towns the authorities would await the official prodding administered by the Municipal Corporations Act of 1835 before taking more effective action.

But far more significant for future development than these early fumblings of urban authorities were the voluntary efforts made in a large number of counties by merchants, gentry, and clergy to protect their properties by setting up associations or by entering into agreements to apprehend and prosecute felons. According to one historian of the movement, there were at least 450 'felons' associations established in England and Wales between 1744 and 1856.[13] The first association of the kind to appear within metropolitan limits was that set up in 1767 bearing the name of the Society for Prosecuting Felons and Forgers; it was followed fifty years later by similar associations formed at Hammersmith and Enfield and, close to the city's borders,

---

11 Radzinowicz, IV, 208–10; See also J. Latimore, *Annals of Bristol in the Nineteenth Century* (Bristol, 1970), pp. 1–7, 187; and D. Large and F. Round, *Public Health in Mid-Victorian Bristol* (Historical Association, Bristol, 1974), p. 1.
12 Edmund M. Gilbert, *Brighton, Old Ocean's Bauble* (Hassocks, Sussex, 1954), p. 196.
13 Adrian Shubert, 'Private Initiative in Law Enforcement: Associations for the Prosecution of Felons, 1744–1856', in V. Bailey (ed.), *Policing and Punishment in Nineteenth-Century Britain* (New Jersey, 1981), p. 25.

at Barnet and West Ham. But in London 'felons' associations remained in short supply; and probably more significant in the history of London policing were the attempts made by a large number of City vestries to set on foot their own quasi-military associations to quell popular disturbance at the height of the Gordon Riots of 1780. On the whole, as they represented an overt challenge to executive authority—they insisted on appointing their own officers indepen- dent of government control—they were met with a stony refusal. But some offers made in the Cities of London and Westminster in a spirit of closer co-operation were well received and the London Military Foot Association of that time has survived in today's Honourable Artillery Company.[14]

Outside London, the establishment of voluntary associations in defence of property appears to have met with a fair response in Sussex;[15] and in Gloucestershire the response was striking and prob- ably as whole-hearted and varied as in any other county. Among the earliest initiatives taken were the agreements signed at Kingswood in 1772 and at Cirencester in 1774, the association formed at Blockley in the same year and, on receiving news of the riots in London, the defen- sive association formed at Gloucester in 1780. But more important per- haps, and certainly more enduring, were the particular measures, taken from the 1770s onwards, by the county's merchants and manu- facturers to defend their properties against both riot and depredation. An early example comes from Bristol, where, in 1777, leading mer- chants combined to raise substantial monetary rewards for the protection of two ships and a warehouse that had been threatened with arson. In 1783, an association of clothiers was set up in Dursley, Wotton, and Uley to prosecute offenders; in August 1802, the woollen manufacturers of the West of England met at Bath to take common action against threats made by their workers to destroy their new machinery and raised subscriptions amounting to £2,500; and, in 1812, a clothiers' association was formed to operate within the county as a whole.[16]

[14] Radzinowicz, II, 211; G. Rudé, 'Some Financial and Military Aspects of the Gordon Riots', The Guildhall Miscellany, no. 6, Feb. 1956, pp. 1–12.

[15] No reference to Sussex appears in either Radzinowicz or Shubert; but, since going to press, I have received from Dr Philips a list of 16 such bodies formed there between 1784 and 1833.

[16] Radzinowicz, II, 116–17; D. Philips, 'Good Men to Associate and Bad Men to Conspire: Associations for the Prosecution of Felons in England 1770–1860', paper read to the Conference on the History of Law, Labour, and Crime held at the University of Warwick, Sep. 1983, pp. 45, 51–3.

Meanwhile, associations of a more comprehensive nature continued to be formed. One of the most successful and most brilliantly patronized was that launched at Tetbury in May 1810, when the participants bound themselves

> to prosecute at their joint Expense, all Persons who . . . should commit any Robbery upon the Person of either of them, or who should feloniously break open or take from the Dwelling-house or any other House of any or either of them, or steal, rob, cut, destroy, maim or damage any of the Goods, Horses, Cattle, Sheep, Lambs, Pigs, Corn, Hay, Timber, or other Trees, Implements in Husbandry, or any other Thing, the Property of any or either of them, within the Counties of Gloucester or Wilts.

Other organizations of a similarly comprehensive, or of a more limited, kind were formed at Kingswood in 1810, Berkeley in 1814, at Slimbridge before 1820, at Bristol in 1824, at Sandhurst before 1830, and at Eastington and Bourn in the 1830s; and an 'Association for the Prosecution of Felons' formed at Dursley in 1795 developed in 1829 into a 'General Association for the Prevention, Discovery and Prosecution of Felonies and other Offences committed within the County of Gloucester'.[17]

Meanwhile, the first decisive step was taken by government to carry through effective reform in the shape of Peel's Metropolitan Police Act of 1829; the new measure created for the first time an all-London force, initially of 3,300 men, intended to *prevent* crime as well as merely to *repress* it and one divorced from the parochial trappings of the past. However, although the new Bill went through Parliament without serious challenge, prejudices against reform were strong and deeply ingrained, based on fears of an imitation of 'tyranny' imported from France and of the encroachment on the traditions and liberties of the old corporations, notably that of the City of London. So it was decided to proceed cautiously. The City was excluded from the new provisions and retained its own force (augmented in 1839 to one of 5,000 men).

In September 1835 it was the turn of chartered boroughs (unchartered boroughs were only brought in later). Under the provisions of the Municipal Corporations Act they were instructed to elect a Mayor, Aldermen, and Borough Councillors, of whom the latter were to appoint a Watch Committee whose duty it was to enrol within three weeks sufficient constables 'to keep the peace by day and night

---

17 Philips, 'Good Men to Associate . . .', pp. 45–53, 60.

to prevent robberies and other felonies and to apprehend offenders'. Yet many large towns—Birmingham and Manchester among them—not being chartered, were excluded from the Act's provisions; others were slow to react; and by 1839 only 198 boroughs were able to claim that they had made a start: they included Bristol, which had set up its force in 1836, with Brighton following in 1838. But forces established were generally inadequate for the purposes stated in the Act: Jennifer Hart has estimated that such municipal forces as had been established by 1856 had little more than half as many police to population as had been provided in London, and she adds that often during this period 'one is much nearer to the old world of the nineteenth-century watchman earning a few shillings by casual police work than in the new world of professional full-time, carefully recruited and supervised Metropolitan police officers'.[18]

The third stage was to enlist the counties; and, after various experiments through rural and parochial authorities, new forces of county-based constabulary, at first on a voluntary basis, were set on foot between 1839 and 1856. Among the first counties to enlist was Gloucestershire (not surprising in view of its long record as a promoter of voluntary association), which established its own constabulary—with a relatively high ration of police to population[19]—in 1839; it was followed by East Sussex (and a dozen others) in 1840.[20] And, finally, by the Police Act of 1856, a further decisive step was taken by co-ordinating the activities of the various regional constabularies under the Home Office in London. So a national system of policing under government supervision—a system that it had been impossible to contemplate in the 1820s and 1830s—gradually came about.[21]

The first recruits to the 'new' police in London—drawn largely from labourers, craftsmen, and ex-soldiers—began to be assembled in May 1830; and, soon after, we find their presence, and their new sense of confidence, reflected in the pages of the Old Bailey *Proceedings*. In August of that year a policeman contemptuously told James Taylor, a cheesemonger who had stolen marked sixpennies and shillings from his master: 'My good man, you made a bad thief to take *marked*

[18] Radzinowicz, IV, 213–15; Jennifer Hart, 'Reform of the Borough Police, 1835–1856', *English Historical Review*, LXX (1955), 411–21 (cit. Radzinowicz, loc. cit.).
[19] Macnab sets the ratio in Gloucestershire in 1846 at 1 policeman to 1,760 inhabitants (p. 283).
[20] Clive Emsley, *Policing and its Context 1750–1870*, pp. 59–75.
[21] Radzinowicz, IV, 252–93.

money.' (To which the prisoner lamely replied 'that he had not looked at it'.) The police continued to use informers as before: Joseph McCarthy, a coiner who passed false coins at a debased rate, was trapped by an informer working for the police and complained in court: 'It is evident that these people will swear to anything'; and, in September 1839, we find the police intervening at an Old Bailey trial to prevent a victim of larceny from recommending a prisoner to mercy —with success, it appears, as the man was transported for seven years. In May 1840 a pickpocket, caught stealing a 2s. handkerchief from Henry Barnes Sawbridge in Hanover Square, complained to the police-man who arrested him: 'Don't drag me in that manner, allow me to speak to the gentleman.' Police brutality was not unknown: when Robert Wendover, a carpenter of Cromer Street, was charged with 'receiving' canary seed, worth 1s. 9d., stolen from a corn-chandler in the Gray's Inn Road, the police (it was reported) smashed open two doors of his dwelling and dragged their prisoner forcibly to the ground. Yet, in direct contrast to such 'overkill', Joseph Morris, of Old Pye Street, Westminster, who was caught red-handed lifting 1s. ½d. from a corn-dealer's shop in Regent Street, escaped prosecution and punishment as he was arrested by 'a very young constable who let him go'.[22]

Yet these examples merely tell us that the presence of the new police soon began to be felt by those most directly involved in crime; it tells us little about their actual contribution to its prevention and containment. How important was it and when did it begin to play a decisive role? It is a question that has been long debated but, not surprisingly, in view of the imponderable factors involved, has yielded no certain answers. For instance, it is known that, in the thirty or thirty-five years following Peel's great reform of the police, crimes of violence, the crimes of juvenile offenders, and the problem of vagrancy (long associated with crime and the so-called 'criminal classes') had begun to fall; and it might be reasonably assumed that the institution of a more highly organized and (after the first teeth-ing troubles in London) of a more efficient police force might have had something to do with this. But, at the same time, it is also known —and perhaps with an even greater degree of certainty—that during the same time the bad economic conditions that blighted the lives of the poor—that major cause of crime—had also eased, from the mid-

22 OB *Proceedings*, 1830, nos. 1592, 1628; 1840, nos. 1450, 1620, 1832; 1850, no. 1068.

or late 1860s at least. So both sets of factors are important; but where do we strike a balance between them and how do we apportion a just measure of credit to them both?

It is a difficult question to answer and I will personally not attempt it; but I am inclined to go along with the tentative judgement expressed by Dr David Jones in a recent paper to the Royal Historical Society (read in September 1982). Dr Jones argues that the new police may be credited with having made three contributions to the prevention and mitigation of crime: (1) Street crimes such as pickpocketing and 'mugging' (a term not then in use) declined with a regular police presence in the streets of the capital. This view, widely subscribed to at the time, was endorsed by the *Edinburgh Review* of July 1852, when it reported that, at the Great Exhibition, there were only eight cases of pocket-picking and ten of pilfering and that in all cases the property stolen had been recovered. This seems further borne out by the fairly rapid disappearance after the 1830s of the pickpocket from the pages of Old Bailey's *Proceedings*.[23] (2) The new police put those most likely to commit crimes—vagrants and the ill-defined and somewhat tenuous 'criminal classes' (to whom I shall return in my concluding chapter)—under constant and stricter surveillance, particularly in areas where 'the propertiless and the propertied rubbed elbows' (to borrow a phrase from another historian cited by Dr Jones). And (3), in the longer term, the police, as they gained in numbers and efficiency, began to exercise a restraining effect as well on those far wider numbers of ordinary men and women whose involvement in crime was occasional and who, even after the 1850s, were frequently faced with economic distress and long or short periods of casual labour or unemployment. The reader may recognize in this category something very similar to those whose crimes I have linked with 'survival'; but that is a larger problem whose solution lies far beyond the confines of the present book.[24]

Finally, an addendum of my own, relating not so much to London as to the provincial or rural scene. It concerns the role of the new police not so much as offering a deterrent to crime or as a crime-

---

[23] Macnab, however, argues that the new police, while effective in restraining minor crimes like vagrancy, drunkenness, assaults, and disorderly behaviour in city streets, had little influence, in the short term at least, in effecting the volume of indictable crime, whether in London, the boroughs or the counties (pp. 243–4, 262–3, 283, 290–2).

[24] D. Jones, *Transactions of R. Hist. Soc.*, XXXIII (1983), 151–68; *Crime, Protest, Police*, p. 139. See also (for *Edinburgh Review*, 1852), Emsley, p. 77.

detector, but rather as a pacifier in civil unrest. In London this was hardly a problem in the forty years following the Napoleonic Wars; even the excitement occasioned by Queen Caroline in 1820 and 1821 led to a bare minimum of arrests for civil disturbance: as we have seen, it was the pickpocket rather than the political protester who created problems for the police. But in the provinces, where social and political disturbance was more likely to occur in this period than in the metropolis, the situation was different and the police acquired a new role to play. This new role had not begun to operate in the labourers' movement we discussed in our previous chapter, but it was success- fully put to the test, in other counties it is true, in the Chartist agitation and riots of the 1840s. The new railway system, emerging in the 1830s, helped to speed the process; and, by the summer of 1842, as Dr F. C. Mather has shown, it was the new combination of troops and stave-carrying police (with the army playing a progres- sively subordinate role) that pacified the northern industrial districts with a relatively minor effusion of blood.[25]

[25] F. C. Mather, *Public Order in the Age of the Chartists* (Manchester, 1959), pp. 154–8.

7

PUNISHMENT

In early nineteenth-century England, there were four possible out-
comes for the prisoner committed for trial at assizes or quarter sessions.
If he was found not guilty or the case not proven, he would be
discharged; and, if found guilty of a felony (without 'benefit of
clergy'), he would be sentenced to death; otherwise he might be transported to an Australian colony for life or for a number of years (this
might be as the result of a reprieve in a case of felony or for the
commission of two or more lesser crimes); or, again, if found guilty
of a 'misdemeanour' rather than a felony, he might be given a prison
sentence of a few days, or weeks or months or years. This was, at
least, the theory; but the final result, or its cause, was never quite so
simple; the actual punishment was rarely made to 'fit the crime', as it
depended rather on a subtle combination of factors, such as the
prevailing state of the law, as determined by Parliament; the interpretation of that law by judges and juries; and (in cases of civil
commotion involving what I have termed 'protest-crimes') the prevailing mood of government, judges and property-owners, in and out
of Parliament, ever sensitive to crimes against property, particularly
in times of emergency.

So let us start with the state of the law regarding capital offences
in the first twenty years of the century, that is before Peel and the
Whig reformers had begun to drastically revise the criminal code. By
the end of the Regency there were over 200 capital crimes on the
Statute Book, most of them left over from the eighteenth century but
with a number of additions made by the later Parliaments of George
III. They included such crimes against persons, property, and State
as murder, piracy, forgery of money or legal documents, shooting with
intent to kill, burglary, robbery, returning from transportation before
expiry of sentence, smuggling with violence, robbery over the value
of £5 (later made £15), private stealing in a shop to a value of £5
or in a dwelling to the value of 40s., rape and forcible abduction,
impersonating pensioners, blackmail through anonymous letters, picking pockets, stabbing and maiming, and stealing cattle or horses or
sheep; and also such real, or potential, 'protest-crimes' as arson, frame-
breaking, threatening letters, riot, 'pulling down' houses or pubs or

shops, shooting at a revenue officers, destroying turnpikes or cloth in the loom, malicious maiming or killing of cattle, and cutting down trees in an avenue (useful for Liberty trees as well as for fuel).[1] The severity of the law at this time in relation to these capital offences is directly reflected in the verdicts of the courts of assize in Sussex and London. Here are a few examples from the Sussex assizes of 1810: in this year William Lamsden was sentenced to be hanged for stealing a gelding, worth £5, and two bay mares (valued respectively at £20 and £15) in the parish of St Clement Eastney; James Garnett was hanged for the burglary of a dwelling house and stealing goods to the value of 36s. (in the case of burglary there was no lower limit); William Treble was sentenced to death for forging a promissory note for £10 after the case had been referred to a committee of twelve judges for a final decision; and James Santer was sentenced to be hanged, following two years' hard labour, for maiming a gelding and three mares by administering poison.[2] Also, strictly in accordance with the law, sentences of death were passed at the Old Bailey in the same year on the following persons for the stated variety of crimes:

1. on William Smith for stealing a sheep worth £3 from a wealthy farmer (owning 270 sheep) on Ham Common on the borders of Surrey;

2. on James Manofie for robbing three silver dollars and 1s. from Alfred Baxter on the King's Highway by force of arms;

3. on John Ingram for stealing a gelding worth £3. 5s. from James Curtis of Highgate;

4. on John Williams for returning from transportation before his sentence had expired;

5. on Ann Riley (though pregnant) for stealing nine yards of printed cotton worth 10s. from Thomas Blower, linen draper, in Tottenham Court Road;

6. on John Whitmore for raping Ann Brown (such sentences were rare);

7. on Timothy Toomey for burglary of John Brooke's dwelling-house at Charing Cross and stealing a gold ring worth £1;

8. on Jacob Flack, servant to Timothy Corner, publican of Leather Lane, for stealing a payment order for £5. 10s. and a £1 note;

[1] Radzinowicz, A History of English Criminal Law, I, 611–59.
[2] Sussex Assizes, 1810, Agenda Bks. 31/21.

9. on Susannah Gerain, of Peter's Lane, St Sepulchre, for issuing
   a counterfeit £1 note, purporting to have been issued by the
   Bank of England;

10. on John Green, a gardener of Harrow-on-the-Hill, for shooting at
    Jane Woodford, a servant, with intent to kill;

11. on John Davis for assaulting John Isbister, a merchant of Blooms-
    bury Square, and robbing him of £2 and a gold watch-key;

12. and on William Tristam, 33, for stealing a silver watch *privately*
    in James Moore French's shop at 75, Fleet Street.

(But Margaret Fitzgerald, who *privately* stole two teapots, a teapot
stand in William Davenport's cutlery and Japan shop in Queen
Street, Westminster, was sentenced to transportation for seven years,
as the value of the goods stolen amounted to no more than 4s. 10d.)[3]

Yet, even at this stage, when capital offences loomed so large in the
court records, the punishment of crime could be relatively mild. This
could happen when the wording of the law (often confusing to the
layman) left loopholes or when the magistrates or juries refused to
co-operate in the literal interpretation of the law. We shall see more
of this in another context; but here it is of interest to cite the example
of Gloucester, where at both assizes and quarter sessions in 1815 (the
earliest year in our sample), there seems to have been a certain
reluctance to apply the full letter of the law to prisoners found guilty
of burglary (an offence, as we have seen, that does not appear to have
caused similar problems to the magistrates and juries of London). At
the Summer Assizes of that year, Joseph Miller, a chairmaker, was
found guilty of breaking into William China's house in Bristol and
stealing his wooden drawers and a large quantity of copper coin; it
was clearly a capital offence, but he was sentenced to be transported
for seven years. The same sentence was passed at the Trinity Quarter
Sessions that month on Francis Berry, a native of Sherstone, in Wiltshire, who in May 1815 broke into John and Hester Merrett's
dwelling-house at Standish and stole a boot, three waistcoats, a pair
of breeches, and other goods. In neither case was there larceny to the
value of 40s., but this, as we have seen, was the limit prescribed for
larceny in a dwelling house without the breaking and entry involved
in a burglary, for which no limit was prescribed. (Or were the
magistrates of Gloucestershire, some of whom were known to be of

[3] OB *Proceedings*, 1810, nos. 153, 165, 186, 187, 267, 290, 302, 411, 425, 549,
564, 819.

a reforming disposition, merely playing innocent or pretending to enforce a limit of their own?)[4]

Similar considerations may have influenced the comparatively lenient sentences passed at that time in Sussex and Gloucester for larceny, riot, rape, and assault. The following examples are taken from the Sussex sessions between 1805 and 1815:

1. When Jane Revol stole four yards of cotton, worth 2s., nine yards ribbon (2s.), and six yards of printed calico (1s.) from John Humwell of Chiddingley, she was fined 1s. and sentenced to a month in jail.

2. William Smart stole a jacket worth 8s., a waistcoat (3s.), and a pair of trousers from John Edwards, a fellow labourer, in Brighton, for which he was jailed for three months and privately whipped.

3. William Bannister, a blacksmith, who riotously assembled 'with other persons unknown' near the workhouse at Fletching in disturbance of the peace, was ordered to pay £50 as surety and to appear at the next quarter sessions at Lewes.

4. When John Sweetman, John Steen, and George McKenzie of Kingston stole nine mallards and ten ducks, worth 19s., from John Woods and James Flood, yeomen of Saltover, near Lewes, they were sent to the House of Correction for three months.

5. James Wick, a brickmaker, was fined 1s. for assaulting James Steyning, a cabinetmaker, of Broadwater.

6. Similarly, when Thomas Note, a labourer, assaulted Catherine Reed of Salehurst (there is no mention here of intended rape), he was fined 1s. and ordered to spend a month in the Lewes House of Correction.

7. But when, in October 1814, Robert Osmont, a tailor, assaulted Charlotte Ranger, of Lewes, 'in order to rape her', he was fined £10 and ordered to spend two months in the House of Correction.

So it looks here as if a clear distinction is being made between assault and assault with the intention (or the actuality) of rape. Yet when, in June 1815, John Brown, a labourer of Piddinghoe in East Sussex, assaulted Henrietta Ford, a minor, 'and raped her' ('did feloniously ravish and carnally know her'), he escaped with one month in the

4 Glos. Pris. Summer Assizes, Trinity QS, 1815.

House of Correction.[5] So, evidently, there was no question here of 'letting the punishment fit the crime'!

So the law was both brutal and full of anomalies; and it was the combination of such factors that prompted reformers, once the Napoleonic Wars were coming to a close, to end their collusion with government and to make a determined effort to change the old penal code. So from 1808 onwards expediency and humanitarian motives combined to strike at the weakest point of all: that is to scale down the number of capital offences. At first it was slow going and a committee of the House, set up in 1819 to recommend reforms, met with ignominious defeat when it proposed amendments to the capital statutes affecting forgery and private larceny in dwelling-houses and shops.[6] So, in 1820, we find the court at the Old Bailey condemning Charles Elliott, a 9-year-old, to death—with no reported recommendation to mercy—for stealing six handkerchiefs worth £1 from a haberdasher's shop in Oxford Street (the inference was presumably burglary, though not stated in the indictment); while Henry Lee and John Thomas Martin were also condemned to death for stealing three coats and a pair of pants (worth £4. 14s.) from a dwelling-house in St John's, Hackney. (But was it a 'non-clergyable' felony after all? For Henry Lee claimed in his defence that their victim, a widow, had sworn at the police office that 'she saw me take the things out of the window'.) And, the same year, four forgers charged at the Old Bailey shared the same fate. They were: Ann Elizabeth Adams, who passed a forged banknote to John Harwood, a grocer of Long Lane, Smithfield; William Paley, a grocer, who issued a false £5 note and passed it to James Aldridge of Clerkenwell; and James Griffiths and William Jennings, who jointly issued three counterfeit £1 notes and passed them to Joshua Boggis and John Adams, butchers of Union Street, St Marylebone.[7]

But the Parliament of 1819, while refusing its Committee's recommendations concerning larceny and forgery, had pledged itself to make reforms; and, by 1820, the death penalty was no longer invoked for picking pockets or for robbing a dwelling-house of goods valued at less than £15; also, in 1820, it ceased to be a capital offence to send threatening letters or to destroy silk or cloth in a loom or frame; the Black Act, which for a century had imposed the death-penalty for

[5] Sussex QS Order Bks., 1810, 1815.
[6] Radzinowicz, I, 549–66.
[7] Proceedings, 1820, nos. 256, 368, 379, 405, 996.

almost every imaginable crime against property, was repealed; and in 1825, it ceased to be a capital crime to assault or obstruct a revenue officer, thus making smuggling a far less hazardous sport. In the court records for 1820 the most noticeable change appears in the sentences passed on pickpockets (for even in Gloucester the law against pocket-picking, unlike burglary, appears to have been enforced to the letter). At the Gloucester Lent Assizes that year, John Roberts, a glover, was transported for life for stealing four £1 notes from the person of John Hall of Bishop's Cleeve. Meanwhile, at the London Assizes the same sentence was passed on three young pickpockets: on John Furzman, 16, who stole a handkerchief worth 2s. from George Douglas Woodfall of Westminster; on William Whaley, 16, for stealing a handkerchief (3s.) from John Barry in Bishopsgate Street; and on William Harwood, aged 14, who stole an even cheaper handkerchief, valued at 1s., from Daniel Deacon in Barbican. (Yet, though an improvement on the sentence of death, the absurdity of this life-sentence on a 14-year-old boy becomes all the more evident when we learn that in the same session, the same presiding judge—the City Recorder—fined Joseph Henry Howell, a boy of the same age, 1s. and discharged him after finding him guilty of stealing a £5 note from his master, John Tucker, a cloth-dresser in the City of London!)[8]

The decisive step forward in the saga of penal reform was taken when Peel began his revision of the code in 1827; this took the bull firmly by the horns by abolishing the death penalty in all cases in which it had become an anomaly and was rarely imposed; and by the transfer the same year of minor crimes against property (such as destroying trees and fences), and those mainly involving juveniles, to the jurisdiction of the justices in petty sessions. But Peel, as in his later reform of the police, was prompted not so much by humanitarian motives as by a desire to make the law more efficient in combating crime; he would certainly have agreed with Samuel Romilly, another pragmatic reformer, that 'the law is nominally too severe, practically not severe enough.'[9] So new Acts were passed defining the death penalty more precisely in the case of other crimes against property. Thus, forgery, on Peel's personal insistence, remained a capital offence (though it was never carried out after 1830) and, as appeared in the

8 Glos. Pris. Regs., Lent Assizes, 1820; Proceedings, 1820, nos. 265, 474, 1239, 1240.

9 Cit. M. Ignatiev, A Just Measure of Pain. The Penitentiary in the Industrial Revolution (New York, 1978), p. 170.

riots of 1830–1, it was still possible for a man to be put to death for breaking machinery (other than threshing machines), for destroying barns or buildings, for burning a haystack, for extorting money with threats, or simple riot; and, in the London assizes of that year, the death sentence was passed (though not imposed) on a clerk who uttered a false money order for £75, and for two cases of burglary in dwelling-houses, in one of which a hatter stole 40 pieces of cloth, worth 6s., while in the other a labourer stole two brooches and an ear-ring, valued at 24s., in each case accompanied, it is true, by a strong plea for mercy from the jury.[10]

But further important changes came with the Whig governments of the 1830s. Capital punishment was abolished for sheep- and cattle-stealing and maiming in 1832 and for house-breaking (or burglary without violence) in 1833; and more capital statutes were repealed by Lord John Russell's reforms of 1834, with simple 'riot' following in 1841 (the notorious and ill-defined 'mobbing and rioting' still survived). By 1840 only eight capital crimes remained, including murder, treason, piracy, burglary, and robbery with violence, and arson of dwelling-houses with persons therein; and, by then, neither machine-breaking nor rick-burning, nor robbery with threats, nor non-lethal assaults (including those on peace and revenue officers)—some of the principal crimes for which protesters (including those of 1830) had been sentenced or put to death in the past—rated as capital offences. In fact, among the more serious 'protest-crimes' previously carrying the death penalty, only two remained: high treason and arson endangering human life; and it was for committing one or other of these that fifteen persons (all but one of them arsonists) were sentenced to death between 1842 and 1848.[11]

But this is not the whole story. The law was one thing and, as we have already noted in places, its application by judges and juries might be something else. This interpretation of the law by the courts was lenient or severe according to the state of the law or to the occasion, or as the pressure of government and public opinion demanded. Early in the century the severity of the law was such that, in cases of capital crimes, juries, when the opportunity arose, tended to give the criminal the benefit of the doubt and were reluctant to find him guilty. This was particularly so where the law provided a monetary limit, as in cases of robbery or larceny in dwelling-houses and shops. Here there

10 *Proceedings*, 1830, nos. 240, 242, 682.
11 Radzinowicz, IV, 330; PP, 1849, XLIV, 58.

were flagrant cases of juries of shopkeepers and craftsmen (as in London) refusing to comply with a law devised by a landlord-dominated Parliament by quite deliberately reducing the price of stolen goods to a third or a half of its stated value.[12] Let us illustrate this point by selecting a few examples from the Old Bailey's *Proceedings* for 1810 and 1820. When in December 1809 Andrew Loader, a Jamaican tailor, was charged with stealing clothes worth 65s. from John Henner, a ship's cook, residing in St George-in-the-East, the jury evaded the death sentence (as prescribed by law) by setting the value of the clothes at 39s. and thus making it possible to impose a 1s. fine and a six-months' term in the House of Correction; and when in April 1820 Ann Wier, a needlewoman of German extraction, colluded with another servant to steal eight silver spoons worth £5. 4s. from her master's dwelling-house, the jury once more set the value at only 39s. so that the prisoner might escape the sentence of death and be fined 1s. and be sent to Newgate for a year.[13]

Moreover, if the prisoner was convicted and sentenced to death on a capital charge, there was, in the days before Peel's reforms, a twelve to one chance (this was, in fact, the average for the seven years 1811 to 1827)—though in the case of forgery it was more likely to be no more than one in five—that the sentence would not be carried out and be commuted for a long term of transportation instead.[14] There were, in addition, several other hurdles to be jumped between the commission of a crime, its detection, and expiation, all of which in the common run of such cases lengthened the odds considerably in favour of the guilty. Fowell Buxton, the penal reformer, in a speech to the Commons in 1819, actually put them as high as a thousand to one. However far-fetched the calculation, it was evident that the law, with its combination of savagery and inefficiency, had fallen into disrepute; and it was this factor, above all others, that weighed so heavily with Peel and other hard-headed reformers. The results of Peel's own contribution in this respect are hard to assess as his new

[12] Some London magistrates were also noticeably more liberal than others (see OB *Proceedings*, 1810, *passim*). This is fairly evident in the case of the City's Common Serjeant when he presided over the Old Bailey sessions in 1810.

[13] *Proceedings*, 1810, no. 102; 1820, no. 215. Other ways in which juries could evade the death penalty, or even transportation for life, was to rule that a given case of pocket-picking was really one of simple larceny (as in 1820, no. 789) or (as in 1820, no. 518) that a lodger, who pledged a sheet at a pawnshop, was entitled to do so, 'the sheet being let to the prisoner with a furnished lodging'.

[14] Radzinowicz, I, 537.

laws were rapidly eclipsed by others; but it appears that, in the years following, severity and leniency were nicely balanced in the judges' interpretation of the law, or applied in varying and vacillating doses. On the one hand the chances in favour of the average convicted felon increased further, as only one in twenty death sentences were carried out between 1828 and 1834 and fewer still in 1836.[15] We have seen, too, how, in 1830, a year of hardship, the court of the Old Bailey often tempered its judgements with mercy in response to prisoners' pleas of economic distress.[16] Yet judges continued to interpret the law with far greater severity when the occasion and the overriding need for stern measures appeared to demand it. The sentences passed on the 'Swing' labourers in the trials of 1830–1, particularly those conducted by Special Commissions at Winchester and Salisbury, are cases in point; and it is also remarkable that where only nine arsonists out of 48 condemned as felons were executed in the comparatively peaceful years between 1820 and 1827, the proportion rose to 47 out of 87 during the tense years of agricultural unrest between 1830 and 1834.[17]

But those were still early days; the real effects of the new liberalization, both in the letter and in the interpretation of the law, only began to be felt by the general run of prisoners committed for trial after 1839. So we find horse-thieves and sheep-stealers being sentenced to prison for terms of twelve and eighteen months at the Gloucester Lent and Summer Assizes of 1840, where they would have been sentenced to death, or at least to long periods of transportation, half a dozen years before; and the Order Books of the West Sussex sessions for the same year record the case of two labourers, who stole sixteen items, including silver spoons, tooth-picks, and pencil cases, worth £20, from a dwelling-house at Arundel: their sentence was to be privately whipped and to spend six weeks with hard labour in the House of Correction. Meanwhile, the Old Bailey sessions were reflecting similar trends: a pickpocket, who stole 5s. 6d. from a grocer's in Strutton Ground, was not sentenced to death or transported for life or for fourteen years, but confined to prison for a six-months' term. The same sentence was passed on John Day, a weaver, who broke into

---

[15] Rudé, *Protest and Punishment*, pp. 66–7.

[16] See pp. 82–4 above; and, in *Proceedings*, see particularly 1830, nos. 318, 410, 434, 446, 556, 636, 742, 920, 940, 1072, 1144, 1212, 1298, 1312, 1372, 1380, 1746, 1752, 2054.

[17] PP, 1847, XLVII, 290.

a bookseller's house at Christ Church and stole 311 books, worth 30s.; and also on Charles Morris, a labourer, who robbed a jeweller's shop of a necklace and a locket, worth £5.[18]

But these were apparently all first offenders. If a prisoner had been previously convicted, even of a comparatively minor offence, no such clemency was shown and his term of jail or exile might be almost indefinitely prolonged. We may cite the case of Thomas Spill, an old man of 77 from the parish of Alveston in Gloucestershire. He was found guilty that same year of stealing two sacks of potatoes from Thomas Bush, a local farmer. Had he been a first offender this would have earned him a short term of prison at most; but, having been given six months for larceny at the previous Epiphany Sessions, he was transported for twelve years; and Henry Carpenter, of Clifton, who stole a bay mare at Old Sodbury, with two previous convictions to his name, was transported for the almost inconceivable term of 30 years. Another case tried at Gloucestershire—this time at the Adjourned Quarter Sessions of 1840—concerned Edwin Rose, a boy of 11 (though he is once described, apparently wrongly, as being thirteen), who was transported for seven years for stealing two loaves from a baker at Cheltenham. But he had been committed three times before and convicted twice: once for stealing two haddocks from a fish-shop in 1838 (when aged 8) and once for stealing a loaf of bread, when aged 9, in 1838. For the first offence he had spent fourteen days in solitary confinement and, for the second, he had been whipped and sent to prison for a week. And now, in 1840, here was this young larcenist, still only 11 years old, whose only crimes were to have stolen food, being sent on the long voyage to Australia.[19]

Yet the general trend by 1840 lay in the direction of a relaxation of the old severity, both through the changes in the law and the greater flexibility in its interpretation by the courts. A major result of these two tendencies was, in the short run at least, to increase the number of sentences to prison and transportation. Since 1788, when Australia was opened as a penal settlement, the most severe penalty, next to death, had been to be sent there as a convict, nominally for life or for a term of fourteen, ten, or seven years (or, exceptionally, as we have already seen, it might be for twelve or 21, or even 30 years);

18 Glos. Pris. Regs., Lent, Summer Assizes, 1840; Sussex QS Order Bks., 1840; *Proceedings*, 1840, nos. 400, 430, 446. But forgers were not shown the same indulgence. John Hencher, who uttered a false money order for £6 to defraud a City tea-dealer, was transported for life (*Proceedings*, 1840, no. 572).

19 Glos. Pris. Regs., Adjourned QS Summer Assizes and Epiphany QS, 1840.

but the actual term made little difference to those wishing to come home as it was rare for a prisoner, having served his sentence, to find the opportunity or the means to return. The numbers of those transported accounted at this time for a considerable proportion of all convictions in the higher criminal courts: about one in three in England and Wales between 1811 and 1834, a little over one in four between 1835 and 1837, and falling to less than one in seven when transportation was beginning to phase out—first in New South Wales and later in Tasmania—in 1847-8. Peel's reforms alone have been held responsible for doubling the numbers of convicts shipped abroad from an annual average of 2,149 between 1824 and 1826 to one of 4,160 between 1828 and 1830; and, in the 1830s, there was a sharp upward turn, as the assizes records for Sussex and Gloucester would testify, in the number of transported sheep-stealers and burglars.[20]

Numbers were further inflated by the numerous death sentences that, in cases of reprieve, were converted to transportation for life or shorter terms. But, to offset this tendency, there were counteracting factors whose influence began to be felt after 1835: among them the growing hostility of Australians to the jailer's role for which they had been cast; and the removal of several minor crimes (including 'protest-crimes') from the list of transportable offences. Poaching, although considered serious enough by Regency landlords and gentry, was one of these: first it was struck from the list by an Act of 1816, except in the case of night-operations; next, in 1828, it ceased to be a transportable offence except for third offenders and where violence was used against game-keepers. We can follow this progression in a few cases from the Gloucestershire records between 1825 and 1835. In 1825, Richard Clarke, a weaver, who had entered a wood at night armed and 'with intent to destroy game', was transported for seven years; in 1831, a shoemaker who had committed an almost identical offence was sent to the county penitentiary at Gloucester for eighteen months; and, at the Lent Assizes in 1835, thirteen men, including a gentleman and a grocer, who had shot and wounded a gamekeeper while poaching at Lasborough, near Wotton, were given varying terms of prison and transportation: the gentleman and the grocer were sentenced to spend a year in the penitentiary and the

[20] A. G. L. Shaw, *Convicts and the Colonies* (London, 1966), pp. 150-7; L. Evans and P. J. Pledger, *Contemporary Sources in British History* (2 vols., Melbourne, 1966-7), II, 90.

rest—ten labourers and a craftsman—to be sent to Australia for life or for seven or fourteen years.[21]

The eclipse of the 'non-clergyable' felony as a capital offence also had the result of creating a larger and more permanent prison population. At a time—as throughout the eighteenth century—when death was considered to be the normal punishment for the majority of crimes against property and persons, the prison had served more as a holding operation providing shelter for prisoners awaiting trial at assizes or quarter sessions; and, except in the case of those unable to pay their debts, it served comparatively rarely as a long-term haven for prisoners once they had been convicted. The principal features of the old-style eighteenth-century Watch House or House of Correction, therefore, were that they were makeshift, dirty, unhealthy, and brutal (they specialized in public whippings for those unable to bribe their jailers); but also they were lax and open to visits by the influential friends of the well-endowed and to prostitutes catering to the needs of those who could afford to pay. In short, the prison, like the penal system on the eve of reform, was both brutal and inefficient.

But, as with the convict ships, once the number of capital crimes had, between 1827 and 1839, been reduced to a handful, far more space had to be found for prisoners sentenced for longer terms. So the penitentiary was born to cater to these new needs and imperatives. Broadly, it was the brain-child of the reforming zeal of John Howard and of the inventive genius of Jeremy Bentham, creator of the first great model prison, the Panopticon. Under such influences the Penitentiary Act was passed in 1779; but the moment for its general application was not yet ripe and would not be so until the arrival on the scene, in the 1820s and 1830s, of Peel and the Whig reformers, the practical advocates of not only a new police and penal system but also of a new prison system, able to respond to new needs and no longer cast in the narrow mould of the landowning legislators of the Parliaments of George III. The first penitentiaries, responding to these new influences and needs, were those built at Gloucester and London: the pioneering Gloucester county jail was completed in 1792; and, in London, the Cold Bath Fields prison followed in 1795 (though its characteristic rule of silence was not adopted until 1834) with Millbank being added in 1816 and Pentonville not until 1842. The

21 Glos. Pris. Regs., Epiph. QS, 1825; Epiph. QS 1831; Lent Assizes 1835. The class bias appears to be evident (see *Conclusions*).

principal objects of the penitentiary, as outlined by Sir William Blackstone, the great constitutional lawyer and an early convert, in a later edition of his *Commentaries*, were to further sobriety, cleanliness (with regular medical inspection), and religious instruction, accompanied by silence and solitude and with frequent periods of solitary confinement, considered conducive to meditation and repentance.[22] (The courts made their own contribution to this new ideology by their frequent incorporation, after the early 1830s, of short periods of solitary confinement of one, two, or three weeks interspersed through a one- to three-year sentence. This accounted for 16.89 per cent of 2,001 cases in the Sussex sessions of 1805 to 1850 and for 6.06 per cent of 3,913 cases in Gloucestershire between 1815 and 1850.)[23]

One further important question remains to consider: why did these changes in the criminal law, in its interpretation and application come about? Was it that the ruling class of the day had to change its rules in order to maintain its hegemony over the labouring and working population which, as we have seen, constituted the mass of prisoners brought to court? Was the criminal law, in fact, essentially an expression of class rule? Both Edward Thompson and Douglas Hay, writing on crime and punishment in eighteenth-century England, have insisted that it was; but they have also argued that, although the rulers manipulated the law and its practice to accord with their own interests, this does not mean that the law, although an expression of class rule, was always unjust. Hay, for example, drawing attention to the increasing number of pardons granted to condemned felons, argues that clemency of this kind was an important concomitant of class rule, for 'mercy was part of the currency of patronage'; and Thompson, for his part, draws attention to a similar paradox: on the one hand that 'the law did mediate existent class relations to the advantage of the rulers'; but that they had to be mediated through legal forms, 'which imposed again and again, inhibitions upon the

---

[22] Ignatiev, A *Just Measure of Pain*, *passim*. The chilling title, well suited to the author's view of the penitentiary, is borrowed from Jeremy Bentham. Michel Foucault, writing in a somewhat similar vein on the 'Carceral Archipeligo' in France (starting around 1840), claims that it was intended to break the spirits (rather than the bones) of the working class and to reduce the delinquents among them to criminal, but socially harmless, morons (*Discipline and Punish. The Birth of the Prison*, New York, 1979).

[23] Coll. W&M CC. Such sentences appear to start about 1835: in London, they are less frequently given and do not begin until 1840.

actions of the rulers'. So, through this 'rule of law', infinitely prefer-
able to the naked rule of arbitrary power, the grosser manifestations
of class became blunted and even the ruled, though having no part
in its creation, could identify with it and even claim it as their own.[24]

Of the penal system as it existed in the bulk of the eighteenth
century—say from the 1740s to the 1790s—the judgement may well
be a just one; and as long as the wars with France lasted, with all the
other problems they raised, the system, though becoming more
objectionable, remained largely unquestioned. But once the wars were
over, and particularly during the late Regency years, the old system
ceased to be acceptable to public oppinion and came under fire both
from within the rulers' own ranks—among those who sat with the
Opposition in Parliament—and from the growing numbers of critics
among merchants, shopkeepers, and craftsmen. This can be inferred
from the reaction of juries to the severity of the law, and we have seen
that even in urban–rural Gloucestershire at the end of the wars there
were magistrates who were reluctant to apply the full rigours of that
law in the case of burglary in their assizes and quarter sessions.

But it was not only that the law was too brutal in its protection of
property. With all its anomalies it had also become inefficient, and
this above all else is what 'bugged' the more thoughtful of the hard-
headed reformers, men like Fowell Buxton, Samuel Romilly, and Sir
Robert Peel. So it was not only the penal code that had to be reformed
but also, and roughly for the same reasons of unacceptibility—
brutality and inefficiency combined—that the old police and prison
systems had to go as well. Broadly, this corresponded to the interests
and ideology of a new class—or, rather, at this time there were two:
the new class of 'interloping' merchants, based on Bristol and the City
of London and engaged in the American and West Indian trade; and
the aggressive manufacturing interests of the towns (Birmingham,
Manchester, Liverpool, and the industrial North); and for such men,
whose interests Peel understood and had very much at heart, the need
was for cleaner and healthier cities, municipal self-government, better
roads, protection of business interests (through tariffs in 1800 but
through freer trade after 1820), and a general overhaul of the system
of justice now that the old one no longer accorded with the interests
of those who were rapidly becoming the new rulers of England.

So, with their new creation, what were the main changes that took

24 Hay, *Albion's Fatal Tree*, p. 45; Thompson, *Whigs and Hunters. The
Origin of the Black Act* (London, 1975), pp. 264–5.

place, say between the 1820s and 1850s? The most noteworthy were the creation of a national professional police, the drastic scaling-down of capital crimes and executions, the removal of indictable offences from the assizes and quarter sessions to the summary jurisdiction of the magistrates' courts, the creation of a more 'modern' prison system, the ending of transportation to Australia (only tolerable as long as an acute shortage of free labour persisted), and the greater flexibility of the courts in interpreting the criminal law. The changes were gradual, but the great leap forward, as we saw, came in the mid-thirties and 1840s.

So have we simply witnessed the replacement of one class system of justice by another; an aristocratic system geared to the land by one created in the image of a commercial and manufacturing middle class? In a broad sense this is probably true, as the old brutality and inefficiency combined (a unique product of the Regency rather than of the eighteenth century itself) had no place in the developing competitive world of the 1840s and 1850s. So a mechanical answer of this kind has a certain merit; yet, as Hay and Thompson found when looking back on eighteenth-century justice (with its hideous product, the Black Act), this simple answer begs too many questions to be quite worth giving. So it was in the 1830s. We might say that as the rulers changed so the penal code and the punishment of crimes, responding to that change, underwent a similar transformation. But this is only a little more than half the truth. Punishment, while adapted to meet the new pressures made by the arrival on the scene of a new set of rulers, was responsive to a wide range of other pressures as well—such as the growth of urban and industrial society, with the tensions that went with it; the demands of an increasingly central and omnicompetent State; the work of humanitarians and penal reformers; changes in public opinion, which could only express itself fully and freely after the Wars; and last (but certainly not least, though often lost sight of), the demand for freer institutions in the old penal settlements of Australia. And all this was further complicated, and its operation delayed, by the resistance to change from other quarters—like the opposition made to the 'new' police by the old corporate municipal interests (the City of London, for example) and (for quite different reasons) by middle-class Radicals and the working-class population of the towns.

8

CONCLUSIONS

WE have seen that crime in the three counties selected for this study followed, in some respects, a common pattern and, in others, displayed significant variations. To start with the variations. We saw that Sussex crime was the most typically rural and that the majority of crimes committed in that county concerned the theft of hay, oats, or firewood, or farmyard animals or clothing, and this in spite of the importance as centres of urban crime of towns like Brighton, Lewes, and Battle. Gloucester, though also a predominantly rural county, turned out to be quite different: we may cite the high incidence of urban crime (for Cheltenham, with its high proportion of resident gentry, far surpassed the record of Brighton in this respect); the relative importance of poaching among its rural crimes; and the significant contribution made to crime by its industrial workers, here at variance with both Sussex and London. Whereas London, differing here from both rural counties, had its own distinctive features: we have seen plenty of examples of the 'inside' jobs performed by maid-servants, shopmen, and lodgers, and the widespread larceny 'from the person' carried out by prostitutes and 'genteelly dressed' young pickpockets.

But we have also noted that all three counties had certain features that they held in common. One was that larceny in its various forms far exceeded all other types of crime, regularly reaching a proportion of 75–80 per cent of all cases tried at quarter sessions in Sussex and Gloucester and, in the London assizes, only falling significantly below this figure in 1850. And, in accordance, in all three counties, even in London, the proportion of violent crimes, whether against property or against persons, was proportionately low. A further common feature we have noted (not surprisingly perhaps) is that criminals tended to be overwhelmingly of the labouring and working classes (though not so consistently in London) and victims to be of the 'middling' or upper classes: most often shopkeepers, merchants, or householders and (in the rural counties) farmers, with a fair sprinkling of gentry, with the labourers and craftsmen (though always in evidence) playing a generally minor role.

But does this tendency of criminals and victims to belong to different, if not opposing, classes in this confrontation mean that, through crime and the combating of crime, they were engaged in a form of class war? To some commentators and to some historians of crime this has appeared as a reasonable proposition; for does not the criminal, as an evident reject from society, attempt, through crimes committed against those most socially favoured, to restore the balance or to climb his way back into his own? It seems a logical and an apparently attractive theory; but, as we have seen in the course of this study, the premiss is a false one. Most conspicuously so in the case of those I have called the 'acquisitive' type of criminal, who, far from turning his back on the norms of the society he lives in, is the one (in my view) who exploits these norms, including the competition for property and profit, in order to enrich himself and become more securely intrenched in a form of society that he patently admires and wishes to belong to. Nor does the proposition hold in the case of those to whom I have attached the label 'survival', those who have generally confessed to or been found guilty of stealing clothing, food-stuffs, fowls, bed-linen, or small amounts of money and who, as so many prisoners appearing at the Old Bailey in certain years have testified, have been impelled to steal, rob, and burgle by economic 'distress'. And here the nineteenth-century evidence appears to con-firm that of the eighteenth, as recorded by two Canadian scholars, Douglas Hay and J. M. Beattie. Hay, as I have mentioned in an earlier footnote (chapter 5, note 1, above), found that such crimes tended to respond directly to short-term economic factors such as a rise in prices or a fall in wages whereas the more serious and more violent crimes, or those most susceptible to capital punishment, were not so responsive to economic motivation;[1] and J. M. Beattie concludes his long essay on 'The Pattern of Crime in England' from 1660 to 1800 with the sentence: 'Crimes against property in the eighteenth century arose primarily from problems of employment, wages and prices, . . . they increased when men found themselves squeezed by rising prices or lower wages or lack of work and declined when they were squeezed no longer.'[2] And this broadly accords with what Marx's collaborator, Frederick Engels, wrote in 1844: '. . . the criminal tables [over the past 37 years] prove directly that nearly all the crime arises within

[1] D. Hay, 'War, Dearth and Theft in the Eighteenth Century', *Past and Present*, no. 95 (May 1982), pp. 111–66.

[2] J. M. Beattie, 'The Pattern of Crime in England 1660–1800', *Past and Present*, no. 62 (Feb. 1974), p. 95.

the proletariat ... The offences are, in the great majority of cases, against property and have therefore arisen from want in some form; for what a man has he does not steal.'[3] But crimes committed for survival, whoever the victim, do not betoken a class war. In fact, from the records we have examined, the only suggestion of a class war was that engaged in by certain participants in unlawful protest: something of the kind might be seen in certain counties during the labourers' revolt against a combination of landlords, parsons, and farmers in the summer, autumn, and winter of 1830; but it is not a clear-cut case and even here we should use the term 'class war' with a certain circumspection.

But, to turn the question round, may the term be applied more appropriately to the attitudes and measures adopted by the possessing classes, or those in authority, to avert, or to protect themselves against criminal acts on the part of the labourers and poor? We have already begun to discuss this question in relation to the vicious code of criminal law adopted by the Parliaments of George III as a protection against poachers, arsonists, and other invaders of property rights during the eighteenth century and the first two decades of the nineteenth. We then saw how when the system was at its most brutal and inefficient it began to break down, partly through the refusal of middle-class juries, notably in London, to co-operate any further with upper-class lawmakers in enforcing savage penalties for relatively minor crimes. So, as we saw, new men, of whom Robert Peel became the symbol, men who were, broadly speaking, from the merchant and manufacturing class, took over from the older generation of rulers and shaped a new penal code, a new policy, and a new prison system.

Was this, then, another form of class rule and were the methods used to exercise it against larcenists and other malefactors cast in the mould of a class war? It is fair enough to say that the new system was the direct expression of a new class system and therefore an expression of class rule. That new system, whose operation we have followed in the three decades from 1830 to 1850, was far more efficient and less indiscriminately brutal, both in intention and execution, than the old; but did it make for a more equitable system of justice? It is doubtful. There was still the presumption that a poor man, particularly one without movable possessions or a home of his own, was a potentially dangerous malefactor who could be detained with

[3] F. Engels, *The Condition of the Working Class in England in 1844* (London, 1952), pp. 130–2.

impunity (I shall return to this point later). Moreover, we have seen cases of gross distortion of justice in the period following Peel's reforms—as in the case of the unfortunate Edwin Rose, sentenced to transportation at the quarter sessions at Gloucester in 1840 at the age of 11 (or was it 13?) for having stolen food on three occasions; and the extraordinary sentences passed at Gloucester Lent Assizes in 1835 on thirteen poachers—nine labourers and a craftsman, a gentleman, and a shopkeeper—all of whom had committed the same offence but who were punished according to their status and occupation, with one year's prison for the gentleman and tradesman and transportation for the rest.[4]

There was something of a class bias, too, though also tempered with economic self-interest, in the selection of prisoners for transportation to Australia. K. M. Dallas, an Australian historian, has argued that the reasons for choosing his country as a place of settlement for convicts were two-fold: to develop a settlement that was strategically well placed for the promotion of Britain's Asian-Pacific trade; and, as the colony developed, to send out shiploads of convict men and women (but preponderantly men) to work as unpaid labour on behalf of the settlers.[5] According to Dallas, the convicts, while originally cast for this role when the First Fleet docked in Botany Bay in 1788, continued to supply this unfree labour until transportation to the Australian colonies ended eighty years later.

While this part of his explanation may not be entirely foolproof, there is evidence enough to lend it some credibility. Most evidently perhaps in the case of the many hundreds of able young pickpockets, mainly boys of 13 to 20 (I do not know the exact number), who were sentenced to transportation in the course of these years, both before 1819, when pocket-picking was still a capital offence (for commutation of the death sentence generally took the form of transportation), and for the twenty or more years that followed. Of course, it would be hard to prove that, in such cases, young men were hand-picked from the dock to provide unpaid labour in the colonies. Yet something of the kind actually took place—or at least was seriously attempted—in the case of 24 of the Gloucestershire labourers transported for their part in the riots of 1830. At their trial in December of that year the

[4] See pp. 112–13 above.

[5] K. M. Dallas, in an unpublished lecture given in Hobart, Tasmania, in 1952; for a résumé, see Geoffrey Blainey, *The Tyranny of Distance* (Melbourne, 1966), pp. 24–6.

chairman of the sessions was Joseph Cripps, who represented the county in Parliament and was also a director of the Van Diemen's Land Company, which owned extensive estates in the north of Tasmania. After sentencing his prisoners, Cripps wrote to the chairman of the Company that they were 'all excellent workmen, strong and useful men', and recommended that they be included among a batch of 50 'agricultural convicts' that he and his fellow directors hoped could be sent together by special ship to Launceston, situated in the north of the island and conveniently close to the Company's estates, where they should be put to work. The chairman wrote accordingly to the Colonial Secretary, outlining the scheme in considerable detail. In the event the plan misfired, having encountered the scruples of the Lieutenant-Governor, Colonel Arthur; yet the intention to subvert justice in pursuit of self-interest was evident enough.[6] But while class justice and discriminatory justice directed against the poorer classes are borne out by these illustrations the deliberate promotion of a class war against prisoners or criminals is not.

Two further questions, not yet considered in this book, remain to be discussed. One concerns the growing volume of crime in urban centres. Is the commonly held opinion correct that crime tends to increase in direct relation to urban growth and most rapidly in cities in the course of rapid expansion? In general, the experience of our three counties would appear to lend some credence to this view. In an earlier chapter we saw that both Brighton and Cheltenham, among the larger towns in our two rural counties, were conspicuous for their steadily rising volume of crime which almost (though not exactly) matched their steadily rising population; and, more generally, if we looked even more closely at the crime records of the two counties we should probably find that, as the century progressed, the ratio of urban to rural crime tended to increase. Yet this correlation between urban expansion and rising urban crime is not a constant one and provides no golden rule. For one thing, the year 1850 (as we found in the case of Cheltenham) was a year in which, while population continued to rise, the number of crimes committed was tending to decline—as it did in Gloucestershire and Middlesex, though curiously not in Sussex, where Brighton continued to expand in terms of both crime and population.

[6] G. Rudé, ' "Captain Swing" and Van Diemen's Land', *Tas. Hist. Assoc.,* XII (i) (Oct. 1964), 12–13, 16–17. See also VDL Co., *Letters-books of Despatches addressed to their Tasmanian Agents* (Tas. RO, Hobart), I, 497–525.

In London the direct opposite was true; if we take its half-dozen most rapidly expanding boroughs (St Pancras, Paddington, Islington, Chelsea, Bethnal Green, and Kensington), each one of which at least trebled its population in forty years, we find that, in every case, while the volume of crime steadily increased up to 1840, it fell noticeably between 1840 and 1850, presumably because more favourable economic factors (and, possibly, the impact of the 'new' police?) had begun to play a counteracting role. Most remarkable, however, is the experience of the City of London 'within the Walls'. Its population remained static (in fact, it was slightly lower in 1850 than it had been in 1810), but its volume of crime (though falling, as elsewhere, between 1840 and 1850) far surpassed that of St Marylebone, the most 'criminal' of the boroughs, in each one of the decennial years and attained a total of crimes, for the whole ten-year sample, of 1,002 against St Marylebone's 460 (see Appendix C at the end of the volume). These two examples—the example of the year 1850 in general and of the City of London in particular—are reminders that, while the rule of a continuous expansion of crime in relation to city growth has a certain general validity, it is not a golden rule, as the intervention of other factors may serve to counteract it.

If this *conditional* validity, however, may apply to crime in general, it appears to have no validity whatsoever—in spite of the arguments of certain authors[7]—in the case of what I have called 'protest' crimes, that is protest engaged in as a breach of the law. To cite the single case of London, a city whose population grew from a little over 800,000 to nearly 2 million in 50 years. Apart from the years 1815 (petitions against the Corn Law), 1820 (Queen Caroline's visit), and 1848 (the third of the Chartist years), London was hardly disturbed by popular protest, whether unlawful (as in the case of some of the Chartist agitation) or not, and I have argued elsewhere that, for the twenty-year period between 1834 and 1853 (such information only became available after 1833), whereas in Lancashire commitments for 'protest-crimes' were 3.2 per cent of commitments for all indictable crimes (with a maximum of 13 per cent in 1842), Middlesex's record of indictable protest remained consistently low: with an average of 0.9 per cent of all commitments for the whole twenty years and a

---

[7] I am thinking in particular of Louis Chevalier, whose book, *The Laboring and Dangerous Classes in Paris in the First Half of the Nineteenth Century* (Eng. trans., New York, 1973) uses arguments that must extend the area of debate from Paris to other large cities of rapid expansion.

maximum of 1.6 per cent in 1848. This is not really so surprising as protest calls for some degree of association which most other crimes do not and is therefore inclined to be inhibited, rather than promoted, by conditions of rapid urban growth. But it is, admittedly, a complicated question and one that I have discussed at greater length elsewhere.[8] So, with apologies to my readers, I will leave the matter there.

I come then to the second, and the last, of my unresolved questions. From the experience of our three selected counties in this period, can one rightly speak of the existence of a 'criminal class', or of 'criminal classes'? This emotive phrase, or its equivalent, has had a long history, going back at least, in the case of London, to Patrick Colquhoun, stipendiary magistrate and founder of the Thames Police Office at Wapping. In his *Treatise* on the London police of his day, Colquhoun claimed that in the London of the 1790s no fewer than 115,000 persons, or one-eighth of its population, were regularly engaged in criminal pursuits: half of them prostitutes or 'lewd and immoral women'; with 8,500 cheats, swindlers, and gamblers; 8,000 'thieves, pilferers and embezzlers'; 4,000 receivers of stolen goods; 3,000 coiners; while 2,500 others preyed on docks and arsenals in the guise of 'Lumpers, Lightermen and Riggers'; and a mere 2,000 were conventional 'Professional Thieves, Burglars, Highway Robbers, Pick-Pockets, and River Pirates'.[9]

From the position that he held Colquhoun might be supposed to be a reliable witness; yet, when stripped of its lurid trimmings, his own account showed that by this time the more violent types of crime—armed robberies, murders, and hold-ups—were on the wane and that his figures were largely inflated by a rising tide of 'economic' crimes and crimes against property. So he can be accepted at best as a very prejudiced witness who, in respect of the 115,000 persons 'regularly engaged in criminal pursuits', has allowed his Gaelic imagination, or his middle-class prejudice, to run away with him. Certainly this is not the picture gained from a study (although, admittedly, a partial one) of the Old Bailey *Proceedings* starting with a year (1810) that follows closely on the date on which he was writing. (Yet he might have found an excuse for his fantasies in the crazy behaviour of the Tory Parliament which, even as the volume of violent crime was declining, were busy adding further capital

---

[8] See my *Protest and Punishment*, pp. 15–21, esp. p. 20.

[9] P. Colquhoun, A *Treatise on the Police of the Metropolis* (London, 1796), pp. vii–xi, 5, 230.

offences to the Statute Book. These stood [according to Colquhoun's own testimony] at 160 in 1795 and had risen to over 200 by 1820.)

So, after the fantasies, which continue, but with the focus of interest no longer being 'receivers', embezzlers, or prostitutes, but rather the vagrants which certainly abounded at this time in every large city, we must ask, what do the court records tell us? Certainly they provide signs of 'professionals'—and not only, though most commonly, in London. At the Old Bailey in 1810 a prisoner, who was charged with stealing a petticoat worth 7s. along with other effects from a Mrs Claxton at Tottenham, called no witnesses to testify to his character (possibly significant) and was described by a police witness as 'a professional thief' and one who 'gets his bread by thieving'. Yet, although he was found guilty, the Common Serjeant (who, admittedly, had a record of leniency) merely sentenced him to be whipped and then to be discharged. And, at the Michaelmas sessions of 1840 at Gloucester, Frederick Woolford, a 21-year-old labourer, was sentenced to be transported for seven years for stealing a pair of boots and a pair of shoes at Cheltenham; but it was not his first offence, as he had already been sentenced to a two-months' term in prison at Michaelmas 1839 and again to a four-months' term in March 1840, on both occasions for larceny; so he had committed three offences in the year between October 1839 and October 1840 and might perhaps have qualified as a 'professional' if his career, cut short by transportation, had been allowed to continue.[10]

More revealing perhaps are the suggestions of a London underworld of crime made in our discussion of 'Criminals' in an earlier chapter. We then read of the case of John Glynn, charged in 1840 with 'receiving' 3 lb. of soap, who was described by Constable G 127 as 'belonging to a notorious gang of thieves' who had been 'several times previously convicted'. Yet the court had clearly no knowledge of his record, as he was transported for the comparatively short term of seven years. In another case we heard mention of a 'Mr Schooley', a professional lock-picker and safe-cracker, and we also became briefly acquainted with the unsavoury John Nash and John Hurley, sentenced to death for burglary and robbing the poor boxes at St Bartholomew's Hospital, of whom one at least was a professional police informer and an *agent provocateur*. And we might add the case of John Grettis, unemployed, who was sentenced to transportation in

10 OB *Proceedings*, 1810, no. 520; Glos. Pris. Regs., Michaelmas QS, 1840.

1820 for assaulting Edward Kelly, a toll-collector at Kilburn, under arms and with intent to rob, and being in the company of a gang of hoodlums, one of whom had already been executed and a second sentenced to be transported (yet the prisoner does not appear to have been very bright: he missed taking his victim's purse which contained £320 in cash!).[11] Such men were no doubt 'professionals' and maybe among those frequenters of London's 'Rookeries' and flash-houses of which Tobias—following Dickens and Mayhew—gives so lurid and dramatic a picture.[12] Yet, according to the records of the Old Bailey at least, they do not appear to have amounted to a great deal; and the notorious parish of St Giles's, so fashionable in the annals of metropolitan crime, appears to have been past its prime as a generator of criminal violence by the 1830s, or by the 1840s at least (see Appendix C).

What of the vagrants who, for some, appear to have been an even richer source of 'professionals' or hardened practitioners of crime? Here the Old Bailey *Proceedings*, and even the records of quarter sessions, are of little use; for vagrants, when rounded up, were most often brought before petty courts of justice or, after 1831 in London, summarily discharged or convicted by a magistrate of the Metropolitan Police. The vagrants certainly presented a problem because of their numbers, though these tended to diminish as the years went by: thus, 9,325 were taken into custody in 1832, 4,437 in 1840, and only 2,700 in 1850; and, in each of these years the magistrate summarily discharged rather less than a half and sentenced the rest to varying terms of detention. These terms, however, do not suggest that these prisoners were taken very seriously by the police as promoters of crime, as they amounted most often to two-to-six weeks or a few days in jail and very rarely indeed (there were two such cases in 1840) were they committed even to quarter sessions for trial.[13] For, after all, their crime was to be poor and have no roof over their heads and maybe to have committed an act of petty larceny; it was not to have robbed a bank, nor did they pose a threat to the established order.

So, after this last rapid survey, my conclusion must be that, even in London, for all its reputation as a centre of professional crime and

---

[11] *Proceedings*, 1820, no. 470; and see chapter 3.
[12] J. J. Tobias, *Crime and Industrial Society in the Nineteenth Century*, pp. 97-121.
[13] *MPCR*, 1832, pp. 8-9, 18-19; 1840, pp. 6-8, 12-14, 18, 26; 1850, pp. 20-1.

'dangerous districts', the case for the existence of a definable 'criminal class' has not been made. There were, no doubt, a minority of hardened criminals and isolated gangs of 'professionals', and perhaps even more 'professionals' working on their own account; but, properly speaking, they were not in sufficient numbers to constitute a 'criminal class'; this may have happened early in the eighteenth century and also, perhaps, in the later years of the nineteenth, but not in the half-century which has been our immediate concern. My findings, in fact, are not so far different from those of David Philips, who, in writing of the Black Country between 1835 and 1860, concludes:

Perhaps 10 per cent of the offences ... were committed by professional burglars, professional pickpockets, experienced thieves. But the great majority of offences seem to have been committed by people who were not full-time criminals, who worked at jobs normally, but also stole articles on some occasions, or became involved in a fight or a robbery.[14]

In the case of the two rural counties—with possible exceptions made for Brighton, Bristol, and Cheltenham and the smugglers at Rye—we should probably exclude the 'professionals' as well, while the existence of a 'criminal class' would be so unlikely as hardly to justify closer investigation.

[14] D. Philips, *Crime and Authority in Victorian England*, p. 287.

APPENDIX

CRIME AND POPULATION
IN THREE COUNTIES

A. SUSSEX

1. Population* and crimes** committed in 25 largest Parishes and Towns 1810–50

Parish/town	1810	1820	1830	1840	1850	Total crimes in five-year sample
Arundel	2,188: 2	2,511: 2	2,803: 1	2,624: 6	2,748: 1	12
Battle	2,531: –	2,852: –	2,999: 4	3,039:16	3,849: 8	28
Brighton	12,012:10	24,429:24	40,634:59	46,666:71	65,569:118	282
Broadwater	2,692: 2	3,725: 2	4,576: 6	5,345: 5	5,970: 4	19
Burwash	1,603: 1	1,937: 2	1,966: 3	1,894: 1	2,227: 3	10
Cuckfield	2,088: 1	2,585: –	2,586: –	2,444: 8	3,196: 3	11
†Chichester	6,452: 2	7,362: –	8,279: 1	8,509: 1	8,647: 2	6
Eastbourne	2,623: –	2,607: –	2,726: –	3,015: –	3,433: 3	3
East Grinstead	2,804: –	3,153: 4	3,364: 5	3,586: 3	3,820: 4	12
†Hastings (inc. St Leonards)	3,952: –	6,185: 1	10,097: 3	11,617: –	17,088: 2	6
Heathfield	1,310: 1	1,613: 2	1,801: 5	1,917: 5	2,208: 3	11
Horsham	3,839: 3	4,575: 3	5,105: 4	5,765:10	5,947: 5	25
Lewes	6,221: 1	7,214:11	8,592:10	9,191:10	10,697: 10	42
Lindfield	1,237: –	1,410: –	1,485: 6	1,939: 3	1,814: 3	12
Mayfield	2,079: –	2,698: 1	2,730: 1	2,943: 3	3,055: 1	6
New Shoreham	770: –	1,047: 2	1,503: 2	1,998: 2	2,590: 1	7
Petworth	2,459: –	2,781: 6	3,114: 3	3,364: 4	3,439: 3	16
Pulborough	1,613: –	1,901: 1	1,879: 4	2,006: –	1,825: 1	6
Rotherfield	2,112: –	2,782: 2	3,056: –	3,036: 2	3,581: 8	12
†Rye	2,681: 1	3,599: 1	3,715: 1	4,031: –	4,592: 1	3
Salehurst	1,653: 1	2,121: –	2,204: 1	2,099: 1	2,191: 3	6
Ticehurst	1,593: 2	1,966: 1	2,314: 2	2,465: 1	2,850: 2	8
Wadhurst	1,815: –	2,136: 3	2,256: 2	2,491: –	2,802: 7	12
Westbourne	1,702: 1	1,852: –	2,031: 5	2,093: 1	2,178: –	7
Worth	1,539: –	1,725: 1	1,859: –	2,423:16	2,475: –	17

2. *Crime Rates in 25 largest towns and parishes in Sussex, measured in terms of population*

Parish/town	Year of highest crime rate	Number of inhabitants per crime
Worth	1850	155
Battle	1840	184
Lindfield	1830	247
Cuckfield	1840	305
Wadhurst	1850	403
Westbourne	1830	406
Heathfield	1840	435
Arundel	1840	437
Rotherfield	1850	448
Petworth	1820	463
Pulborough	1830	495
New Shoreham	1820	502
Brighton	1850	556
Horsham	1840	594
Burwash	1830	654
Lewes	1820	656
East Grinstead	1830	673
Salehurst	1850	703
Broadwater	1830	762
Ticehurst	1850	797
Mayfield	1840	981
Eastbourne	1850	1,014
†Rye	1810	2,681
†Chichester	1810	3,212
†Hastings (inc. St Leonards)	1830	3,366

* Population figures from *Victoria History* of Sussex (London, 1907), pp. 217–28.
** Crime figures from Sussex RO, QS Order Bks., 1810–50.
† Rye, Hastings and Chichester had their own courts of quarter sessions, the first two as Cinque Ports. The cases tried in them are not included in the County QS.

B. GLOUCESTERSHIRE: MAJOR PARISHES AND TOWNS

1. Population and crimes, 1820–50*

Parish/town	1820	1830	1840	1850	Total crimes in ten-year sample
Berkeley	3,835: 3	3,396: 6	4,405: 10	4,344: 9	28
Bisley	1,548: 12	1,642: 10	1,944: 23	2,117: 12	57
Bitton	5,421: 27	5,896: 13	5,339: 30	4,801: 8	78
**Bristol (City & County)	52,888: 20	59,074: 29	64,266: 24	65,722: 17	90
Cam	1,885: 2	2,071: 1	1,851: 6	1,650: 13	22
Charlton Kings	1,607: 3	2,478: 11	3,232: 11	3,174: 3	28
Chipping Campden	1,798: –	2,038: 2	2,087: 2	2,351: 4	8
†Cheltenham	13,396: 73	22,942:169	31,411:205	35,051:127	574
Cirencester	4,987: 1	5,420: 28	6,014: 24	6,014: 24	77
‡Clifton	8,811: –	12,032: 8	14,177: –	17,625: –	8
Dean Forest	5,535: –	7,014: 3	10,692: –	13,566: 22	25
Dursley	3,186: –	3,226: 8	2,931: 8	2,752: 1	17
Gloucester	9,744: 10	11,933: 22	14,152: 30	16,051: 21	83
Fairford	1,547: 7	1,574: 20	1,672: 3	1,859: 11	41
Hawkesbury	1,834: 1	2,182: 3	2,231: 2	2,185: 2	8

Horsley	3,565: 7	3,690: 12	3,064: 12	2,931: 5	36
King's Stanley	2,269: 6	2,438: 16	2,200: 15	2,095: 16	53
Lydney	1,393: –	1,534: 2	1,885: –	2,597: 1	3
Mangotsfield	3,179: 3	3,508: –	3,862: 4	3,967: 1	8
Minchinhampton	4,907: 13	5,114: 12	4,899: 16	4,469: 10	51
Moreton-in-Marsh	1,015: 16	1,331: –	1,395: 4	1,512: 30	50
Newent	2,660: 10	2,851: 19	3,099: 25	3,306: 7	61
Newland	3,383: –	4,048: 3	4,085: 4	4,574: 6	13
Painswick	4,044: 36	4,099: 73	3,730: 14	3,464: 11	134
Rodborough	2,038: 2	2,141: 3	2,147: 2	2,208: 1	8
Stapleton	2,137: 8	2,715: 12	3,944: 11	4,849: 6	37
Stonehouse	2,126: 6	2,469: 14	2,755: 7	2,598: 6	33
Stow on the Wold	1,731: –	1,810: 3	2,140: 2	2,250: 2	7
Stroud	7,097: 32	8,607: 44	8,680: 54	8,798: 27	157
Tetbury	2,734: 4	2,939: 5	2,982: 24	3,325: 4	37
Tewkesbury	4,962: 4	5,780: 2	5,862: –	5,878: 3	9
Thornbury	3,760: 1	4,378: 5	4,706: 3	4,614: 7	16
Westbury on Severn	1,859: 4	2,032: 12	2,225: 19	2,498: 27	62
Westbury on Trym	3,721: 18	4,263: 15	6,728: 24	6,728: 14	71
Winchcombe	2,240: 3	2,514: 17	2,613: 5	2,824: 7	32
Winterbourne	2,627: 6	2,889: 4	3,151: 4	2,876: 2	16
Wotton-under-Edge	3,286: 30	5,482: 17	4,702: 20	4,224: 19	86

2. *Major Gloucester parishes and towns 1820–50; crime rates in the most 'criminal' year in relation to population**

Parish/town/city	Year of highest crime rate	Number of inhabitants per crime
Moreton-in-Marsh	1850	50
Painswick	1830	55
Fairford	1830	79
Bisley	1840	85
Wotton-under-Edge	1820	109
Tetbury	1840	124
Cam	1850	127
King's Stanley	1850	131
Newent	1840	131
Cheltenham	1830	136
Winchcombe	1830	148
Stroud	1840	161
Stonehouse	1830	176
Bitton	1840	178
Cirencester	1830	193
Charlton Kings	1830	225
Stapleton	1830	226
Horsley	1840	255
Minchinhampton	1840	300
Dursley	1830	366
Gloucester	1840	472
Chipping Campden	1850	588
Stow on the Wold	1830	603
Dean Forest	1850	617
Mangotsfield	1840	965
Newland	1830	1,021
Tewkesbury	1820	1,240
‡Clifton	1830	1,504
**Bristol	1840	2,035

* *Sources*: for *population*: VCH, *Gloucestershire*, II, 175–87;
         for *crimes*: Glos. Pris. Regs. 1820–50.
** *Bristol*: see also note 11 to chapter 2.
† *Cheltenham's* attraction for criminals may be largely explained by the wealth and status of its residents: there were over 1,000 gentry residing in the town in 1850 (*Edwards's Directory of Cheltenham*, 1850).
‡ *Clifton* was incorporated with Bristol before 1841 census.

C. CITY OF LONDON AND MAJOR METROPOLITAN PARISHES

*1. Population and crimes committed in major parishes, 1810–50**

	1810	1820	1830	1840	1850	Total crimes in ten-year sample
Edmonton Hundred						
Edmonton	6,824: 3	7,900: 2	8,192: 2	9,027: 4	9,708: 2	13
Enfield	6,636: 1	8,227: 8	8,812: 12	9,367: –	9,453: 8	29
Tottenham	4,771: 4	5,812: 3	6,937: 6	8,584: 8	9,120: 2	23
Elthorne Hundred						
Hillingdon	4,663: 1	5,636: 2	6,885: –	9,246: 6	9,588: –	9
Finsbury Div.						
Clerkenwell	30,537: 9	39,105: 24	47,634: 34	56,756: 34	64,778: 12	113
Islington	15,065: 9	22,417: 29	37,316: 38	55,699: 64	95,329: 26	166
St Luke	32,545: 29	40,876: 25	46,642: 32	49,829: 34	54,055: 10	130
Holborn Div.						
Hampstead	5,483: 1	7,263: 6	8,588: 38	10,093: 12	11,986: 6	63
Paddington	4,609: –	6,476: 5	14,540: 10	25,173: 18	46,305: 6	39

1. *Population and crimes committed in major parishes, 1810–50**

	1810	1820	1830	1840	1850	Total crimes in ten-year sample
St Andrew Holb.	23,971 : 27	26,492 : 33	27,334 : 46	27,438: 32	23,355: –	138
St George Mart.	: 1	: –	: 4	7,897: 4	8,763: –	9
Saffron Hill	7,482: 9	9,270: 2	9,745: 10	9,455: 10	8,728: 2	33
St Giles in Fields	34,672: 14	57,793 : 12	36,932: 20	37,311: 18	37,407: 6	70
St George Bl'b'y	13,864: 11	: 12	16,475: 40	16,981: 28	16,807: 6	97
St Marylebone	75,624: 56	96,040: 46	122,206:150	138,164:150	157,696: 58	460
St Pancras	46,333: 33	71,838: 47	103,548: 60	129,735: 90	166,956: 28	258
Kensington Div.						
Chelsea	18,262: 8	26,860: 10	32,371: 16	39,896: 34	56,185: 14	82
Chiswick	3,892: –	4,236: 2	4,994: 6	5,811: 8	6,303: 4	20
Ealing	5,361: –	6,608: 2	7,783: 10	8,407: 12	9,828: 2	26
Fulham	5,903: 1	6,492: 2	7,317: 2	9,319: 8	11,886: 6	19
Hammersmith	7,393: 1	8,809: 2	10,222: 14	13,453: 6	17,760: 12	35
Kensington	10,886: 11	14,428: 7	20,902: 46	26,834: 40	44,053: 14	118

Tower Div.

Bethnal Green	33,619: 12	45,676: 10	62,018: 18	74,088: 36	90,193: 4	80
Bromley	3,581: -	4,360: -	4,846: 2	6,154: 8	11,789: 2	12
Hackney	16,771: 5	22,494: 13	31,047: 60	37,771: 60	53,589: 16	154
Limehouse	7,386: 15	9,805: 8	15,695: 10	21,121: 14	24,561: 14	61
Poplar	7,708: 9	12,223: 1	16,849: 4	20,342: 2	28,384: 10	26
St George in East	26,917: 6	32,528: 7	38,505: 4	41,350: 14	48,376: 2	33
Shadwell	9,855: 6	9,557: 7	9,544: 6	10,060: 30	11,702: 4	53
Shoreditch	43,930: 12	52,966: 23	68,569: 20	83,432: 30	109,257: 10	95
Spitalfields	16,200: 10	19,650: 12	17,949: 18	20,436: 10	20,960: 8	58
Stepney	27,991: 29	36,949: 34	51,023: 26	63,723: 18	80,218: 22	129
Wapping	3,313: 18	3,078: 7	3,564: 26	4,108: 16	4,477: 14	81
Whitechapel	27,578: 20	29,407: 17	30,733: 24	37,053: 18	37,848: 30	109

City of London

Within the Walls	19,327:146	19,530:126	19,139:308	19,055:280	19,307:142	1002

City of Westminster

St Anne Soho	12,288: 16	15,215: 6	15,600: 22	16,480: 32	17,335: 14	90
St Clement Danes	13,706: 5	14,763: 7	15,442: 14	15,459: 10	15,550: 10	46
St George Han. Sq.	41,687: 18	46,384: 25	58,209: 20	66,736: 30	73,458: 8	101
St James West.	34,093: 20	33,819: 20	37,053: 18	37,426: 40	36,406: 16	114
St John Evan.	10,615: 5	16,835: 8	22,648: 16	26,223: 34	34,295: 12	75
St Margaret	19,027: 11	22,387: 16	25,344: 12	30,258: 8	30,942: 6	53
St Martin in Fields	26,585: 13	28,252: 19	28,732: 20	24,917: 38	24,461: 10	100
St Paul Covent Gard.	4,992: 21	5,304: 42	5,834: 52	5,718: 38	5,810: 28	181

2. *Major metropolitan parishes, 1810–50: crime rates in most 'criminal' year in relation to population—in descending order of magnitude**

Parish/city	Year of highest crime rate	Number of inhabitants per crime
City of London	1840	64
St Paul Covent Garden	1830	112
Wapping	1830	137
Hampstead	1830	226
Shadwell	1840	335
St George Bloomsbury	1830	412
Kensington	1830	454
Limehouse	1810	492
Hackney	1830	501
St Anne Soho	1840	515
St Andrew Holborn	1830	594
Ealing	1840	700
Chiswick	1840	726
Hammersmith	1830	730
Enfield	1830	734
Bromley (by Bow)	1840	759
St John Evangelist	1840	771
St Marylebone	1830	801
Saffron Hill	1810	831
Poplar	1810	856
Islington	1840	870
St James Westminster	1840	936
Stepney	1810	963
Spitalfields	1830	997
Tottenham	1840	1,073
St Clement Danes	1830	1,103
St Luke	1810	1,122
Fulham	1840	1,165
Chelsea	1840	1,167
St Martin in the Fields	1830	1,186
Whitechapel	1850	1,261
St Margaret	1820	1,399
Clerkenwell	1830	1,401
St Pancras	1840	1,442
Paddington	1830	1,454
Hillingdon	1840	1,541
St George Hanover Sq.	1820	1,831
St Giles in the Fields	1830	1,847
St George the Martyr	1840	1,974
Bethnal Green	1840	2,060
Shoreditch	1840	2,781
St George in the East	1840	2,954

* Sources: OB *Proceedings*, 1810–50; VCH, *Middlesex*, II, 112–19.

BIBLIOGRAPHY

I. PRIMARY SOURCES

1 *Public Record Office, London*

Assizes: South-Eastern Circuit (Sussex) 1810–50. Agenda Books 21, 23, 26, 28, 32; Calendars of Prisoners, 1830–50 (printed).

2 *County Record Offices*

East Sussex (Lewes) and West Sussex (Chichester): QS Order Books, 1805–50; Recognizances, 1820–35. Rye Borough Court Sessions Books 1772–1828, Indictments 1801–39 (Lewes); Chichester City Court of QS, rolls 1804–34 (Chichester).

London: QS records: rolls, 1805–50; examinations and depositions (part. 1850); printed Calendars of Prisoners, 1846–50. Newgate Calendars of Prisoners awaiting trial at OB sessions 1820–50 (OB/CB vols. 1, 4, 9, 17, 18).

Gloucestershire: Q/Gc: Gaol Calendars, 1815–71 (here referred to as Gloucester Prison Registers); Q/SZB: Registers of Recognizances, 4 vols., 1805–35; Q/SIa: five-year sample of indictments, 1840–60.

Bristol: QS records: Sessions Dockets, 1810–50; Bristol Police: Record Book 1836–77; Occurrence Books, 1836–38, 1838–1839, etc.

3 *Guildhall Library, City of London*

Old Bailey Sessions Papers: *The Whole Proceedings in the King's Commission of the Peace . . . 1707–1913* (printed).

4 *Library of New Scotland Yard*

Printed volumes of Metropolitan Police Criminal Returns (MPCR), 1831–92.

5 *Hastings Museum*

Records of the Town and Port of Hastings, vols. 1–3, 1779–1828 (QS minutes; defective).

6 *Parliamentary Papers*

Criminal Returns XL (1835), XXXVIII (1840), XXXVII (1845), XLVII (1847), XLV (1850), XLIII (1854–5).

7 *Printed Collections, Directories, Dictionaries*

Australian Dictionary of Biography (Melbourne).
Dictionary of National Biography (London).
Edwards's Cheltenham Directory, 1850.
Directory of Bristol, 1850.

8 *Contemporary Comment*

COLQUHOUN, Patrick, *A Treatise on the Police of the Metropolis* (London, 1796).

II. SECONDARY WORKS

1 *Books and Articles*

BEATTIE, J. M., 'The Pattern of Crime in England 1660–1800', *Past and Present*, no. 62 (Feb. 1974), pp. 47–95.

BLAINEY, G., *The Tyranny of Distance* (Melbourne, 1966).

DUNBABIN, J. P. D., *Rural Discontent in Nineteenth-Century Britain* (London, 1974).

EMSLEY, C., *Policing and its Context 1750–1870* (London, 1983).

FOUCAULT, M., *Discipline and Punish: The Birth of the Prison* (New York, 1979).

GATRELL, V. A. C. and HADDEN, T. B., 'Criminal Statistics and their Interpretation', in E. A. Wrigley (ed.), *Nineteenth-Century Society* (Cambridge, 1972), pp. 336–96.

HAY, D., LINEBAUGH, P., THOMPSON, E. P., *et al.*, *Albion's Fatal Tree: Crime and Society in Eighteenth-Century England* (London, 1975).

—— 'War, Dearth and Theft, in the Eighteenth Century', *Past and Present*, no. 95 (May 1982), pp. 117–60.

HOBSBAWM, E. J. and RUDÉ, G., *Captain Swing* (London, 1969).

HUGH, Mike and MAYHEW, P., *The British Crime Survey. First Report.* HO Research Study no. 76, HMSO (London, 1983).

IGNATIEV, M., *A Just Measure of Pain: The Penitentiary in the Industrial Revolution* (New York, 1978).

JONES, D., *Crime, Protest, Community and Police in Nineteenth-Century Britain* (London, 1982).

—— 'The New Police, Crime and People in England and Wales 1829–1878', *Transactions of the Royal Historical Society*, XXXIII (1983), 151–68.

MAYHEW, H., *London Labour and the London Poor* (London, 1864; repr. 1961–2).

PETROVITCH, P., 'Recherches sur la criminalité à Paris dans la seconde moitié du XVIIIe siècle', in *Cahiers des Annales* 33 (Paris, 1971), pp. 187–261.

PHILIPS, D., *Crime and Authority in Victorian England, The Black Country 1835–1860* (London and New Jersey, 1977).

RADZINOWICZ, L., *A History of English Criminal Law and its Administration from 1750* (4 vols., London, 1948–68).

ROBSON, L. L., *The Convict Settlers of Australia* (Melbourne, 1965).

RUDÉ, G., 'Protest and Punishment in Nineteenth-Century Britain', *Albion*, V (1973), 1–23.

—— 'Captain Swing and Van Diemen's Land', *Tas. Hist. Assoc.*, XII (1964), 6–24.

—— *Protest and Punishment: The Story of the Social and Political Protesters transported to Australia* (Oxford, 1978).

STEVENSON, J. (ed.), *London in the Age of Reform* (Oxford, 1977).

SHAW, A. G. L., *Convicts and the Colonies* (London, 1966).

STORCH, J. D., 'The Plague of the Blue Locusts. Police Reform and Popular Disturbance in Northern England 1840–67', *International Review of Social History*, XX (1975), 61–90.

THOMPSON, E. P., *Whigs and Hunters. The Origin of the Black Act* (London, 1975).

TOBIAS, J. J., *Crime and Industrial Society in the Nineteenth Century* (London, 1967).

Victoria County History: Gloucestershire (11 vols., London, 1907–80); *Middlesex* (7 vols., 1911–82); *Sussex* (9 vols., 1905–82).

ZEHR, H., *Crime in the Development of Modern Society* (London, 1976).

2 Theses

MACNAB, K. K., 'Aspects of the History of Crime in England and Wales between 1805 and 1860' (unpub. D. Phil., University of Sussex, 1965).

JERRARD, B. C., 'The Gloucestershire Police in the Nineteenth Century' (M. Litt., University of Bristol, 1977).

GENERAL INDEX

SELECT INDEX
OF CRIMINALS AND VICTIMS*

I. CRIMINALS

*ES = East Sussex   WS = West Sussex

II. VICTIMS